Just So You Know

Essays of Experience

Hanan Issa is a Welsh-Iraqi writer who explores narrative history and the ways we connect in her writing. She has collaborated with platforms including BBC Wales, Film4, Bush Theatre, Hay Festival, National Museum Wales, Artes Mundi, StAnza festival, Lumin Journal, and Literature Wales. She is the co-founder of the Where I'm Coming From open mic and her debut poetry pamphlet 'My Body Can House Two Hearts' is published by Burning Eye Books.

Durre Shahwar is a writer, editor, and co-founder of Where I'm Coming From, an open mic that platforms under-represented writers in Wales. Durre has contributed to various anthologies including *Know Your Place: Essays on the Working Class* (Dead Ink Books), *We Shall Fight Until We Win* (404 Ink), *Homes For Heroes 100* (Bristol Festival of Ideas). Her work explores the theme of identity in all its forms. She is a regular speaker and performer at events. Shahwar was the recipient of a Literature Wales Writers' Bursary and has been part of the Hay Festival Writers at Work scheme, as well as BBC Writersroom Wales. She is currently doing her PhD in Creative Writing at Cardiff University and working towards her first book and play.

Özgür Uyanık is an author, screenwriter and film director whose family emigrated from Turkey to the United Kingdom. He is a Creative Writing PhD candidate at Cardiff University and has an MA in Creative Writing and English Literature. His debut novel *Conception* (Fairlight Books) is out in 2020 and he currently has several screenplays in development with support from by Ffilm Cymru Wales and the BFI.

Just So You Know
Essays of Experience

Edited by
Hanan Issa, Durre Shahwar
and Özgür Uyanık

Parthian, Cardigan SA43 1ED
www.parthianbooks.com
First published in 2020
ISBN 978-1-912681-82-2 paperback
ISBN 978-1-912681-83-9 ebook
Project Editor: Kathryn Tann
Cover design by Syncopated Pandemonium
Typeset by Elaine Sharples
Printed by 4Edge Limited
Published with the financial support of the Books Council of Wales
British Library Cataloguing in Publication Data
A cataloguing record for this book is available from the British Library.

Contents

Notes from the Editors

When I was approached by Parthian to co-edit and contribute to an anthology of essays from so-called "marginalised voices", I was excited to be involved in a project where the brief was sufficiently unconstrained that I felt confident the project would seek to capture as many voices as possible from a wide-ranging variety of backgrounds.

The concept was to facilitate these voices being heard on their own terms without prescribing too many parameters. Hence, the remit requested *creative* essays with no restrictions on style or content. The resultant collection therefore – we hoped – would contribute implicitly to challenge many of the tropes and assumptions that accompany definitions of under-represented writers in the literature.

In these pages then, the reader can discover the self-reflective creative essays that were finally selected, which are both sincere and authoritative – the very definition of authentic. They explore distinct and absorbing topics from an extensive array of compelling viewpoints such as self-identity, erasure of heritage, Welsh language and culture, the immigrant experience as well as problematic notions of the other by BAME, LGBTQ+, neurodivergent and disabled writers confronting heteronormative and neurotypical ideals.

Sometimes the stories that frame the essays begin in far away places like Uganda, Pakistan, Iraq or the Caribbean and have found their way to Wales in one fascinating way or another. There are essays that read like beguiling prose poetry, those that conform to a stricter notion of the form and almost everything else in between. However, all of them bring fresh perspectives and a wealth of thought-provoking insight from writers who have been given the space here to be heard and share their experiences.

– Özgür Uyanık

While putting together the call out for this anthology we, the editors, were meticulous with our word choices. We wrestled with choosing a term that would properly specify the type of writers we were looking for: 'Underrepresented'; 'marginalised'; 'unheard voices' were all discussed at length. Eventually we agreed that the term needed to be expanded and, to avoid confusion, we listed the specific demographics we were targeting.

After the deadline had passed I approached several writers that I had hoped would submit but hadn't. Alongside the usual reasons such as a busy workload or lack of inspiration to write, a few people had taken issue with the wording of the call out itself. For me, that experience reinforced how inadequate the terms listed above (including the definition we chose) really are. The breadth and scale of human emotion and experience captured in these pieces channels a spectrum so vast and beautifully unique it seems somehow disrespectful to even try pigeonholing them all under one heading.

As we began reading the pitch submissions it became clear that we had been gifted with a plethora of insightful perspectives not often afforded a platform. The process of editing was a collaboration between the writers and us editors to work out the best way of showcasing the voice and story of each essay. This meant that, for some pieces, it felt more appropriate for them to be structured like a traditional essay whereas others opted to explore themes and ideas via a more creative route.

The result is this vibrant collection of strong voices expressing themselves devoid of the burden to explain, conform, or pander to those that do not necessarily share their outlook. The *Just So You Know* writers are unapologetically commanding our attention and we would do well to sit up and take notice.

– *Hanan Issa*

Anthologies of creative non-fiction essays that seek to highlight underrepresented topics such as race, religion, LGBTQ+, and neurodiversity (to name a few) like this one does, often mention the current political and social context in which they are written. But more often than not, that current political and social context, while referring to the UK as a whole, isn't quite inclusive of Wales and Welsh voices. Which is why, when approached to edit this anthology, I was excited from the beginning about its potential.

Through the callout we drew in a range of voices and experiences; learning to ride a bike and embracing who you are as a mixed-race, autistic, dyspraxic and dyslexic person, a portrayal of bi-polar disorder through fairy tale and Taoism, a parallel between Welsh and Kenyan mythologies and the depiction of violence and women in folk tales, a half-Filipino half-Pakistani woman exploring her ancestral connections through fabrics, an exploration of language as water as a multi-lingual Welsh speaker and so much more.

Each author's individual journey is stoic, uplifting, nuanced and inspirational. Told through different writing styles, we're fortunate to have an insight into each one of them. These are strong Welsh voices that are unapologetic and don't pander to stereotypes of what a Welsh experience should look like to the outside eye. And what's more is that this is just a sample of the stories that are out there. There is space and potential for each of these underrepresented topics to have an anthology of their own, written solely by Welsh authors. We can only hope that by creating this, others are encouraged to continue the conversation.

Because, just so you know, these voices exist.

– *Durre Shahwar*

I, Invisible Immigrant

Derwen Morfayel

I examine the word 'marginalised', trying to decide whether I interpret it as excluded or overlooked. The latter sounds unintentional, the way lifelong friends continue to mispronounce your name and at the same time love you very much. I consider what it means to be a margin. At its worst, it is empty space, and at its best, it is the frame of a text. I am sitting on a margin and from there I can better read the page. I can look into the pool of words as a whole.

This topic is significant in light of the settled Europeans who are right now in an inconclusive situation, sidelined during a crucial time that makes us question our place within our community. Distinctions regarding birthplace have been emphasised in people who were, until recently, comfortably immersed in their British lives.

Cultural identity is not limited to what your passport dictates. However, like any relationship, your commitment and connection to a culture can depend on how it treats you back.

In my fiction I often create characters that are in constant emotional transit with regards to identity, not unlike an

1

immigrant. My own experience trails after me still, even in my creative writing.

For an immigrant who is lucky to have positive experiences that outweigh the bad, I find myself on this border temporarily, transiting to and from and beyond it at times when my British and Spanish identities are questioned by others or even myself. There was a particular line in the guidelines for this project that is relevant here because it invited writers who are born in, living in, or have a connection to Wales. It suffices to say this is not always the case in calls for writers within certain communities, and 'writers *from*' can sometimes exclusively refer to 'writers *born in*'. It is almost as though what they really want to ask is 'Is this the "land of your fathers" or not? With the UK going through significant changes, I have become more appreciative of publications that allow me to self-identify as Welsh or British.

Recent events have shone a light on the fact that, like most settled Europeans, I had no voice in a referendum that affects me in more ways than one. When the subject came up, I was met with surprise and appalment by people who believe it makes more sense to take part in all elections and referendums of the country you are a long-term resident in and directly affected by. It is a minor curse of the immigrant that others are unaware of the rights you do and don't have. 'What do you mean you can't vote?' Depending on the country you were born in, you might not be able to obtain dual nationality to resolve this. Furthermore, not everyone can afford to go through the entire process of changing their nationality – the cost being a common barrier for many working class people. Personally, I would say that full voting rights are the main social handicap I have experienced and therefore the essential motive for a citizen to do this but not

2

everybody wants to for reasons ranging from practical to emotional. I can understand the two sides to this argument equally: that it makes sense for the residents of a country to elect in everything that affects them, *and* it makes sense for only citizens to vote in matters to do with the country they are nationalised in. The fact is that at times of division and of breaking ties, a familiar idea surfaces again: this place we are closest to is not letting us come any closer.

I am writing from the position of a person who did all their growing up outside their birth country. A passive immigrant if you will. That is to say, similarly to language acquisition, I did not learn this culture as an adult trying to piece out its logic; I assimilated it as a child and it was blended softly into my early years. My experience may ring bells for many immigrants with varying personal circumstances, who have been influenced by more than one culture in a significant way. The picture is more or less as follows: you reach a point where your current environment overrides the small portion you know about your country of origin. Your parents' words, visits to the motherland if you are so lucky, foreign channels through which you learn of the macrocosm that is your foreign side. You do not forget but you clean out to make room for all your Britishness. After all, you understand the social references better, its humour and punctuated politeness, please and thank you. In my particular amalgamation of cultures, I knew not to kiss my British friends as often as I would my Spanish ones. I was quiet on buses and when people spoke too loudly, looked around me awkwardly. (I really miss the word 'awkward' in Spanish; *incómodo*/uncomfortable just doesn't get the right feeling across. Awkward sounds like something you wedge in a door to overhear an inappropriate conversation.) I said sorry even when it was someone else who had bumped into me. I still do.

To belong to more than one place can mean never feeling at home in one more than the other. You are always missing something.

Nan is getting old.

Friends are confused about the skin colour you should tick on forms. Are you sure you're white? Is it tanned or is it permanent?

Grandad is getting sick.

Your aunt had a baby.

Remember to read a bit in both languages to practise!

Your cousins grew up.

Why are you mixing English words? Uh, that's just the way I think.

Sorry.

Your friends had the best time last summer while you were away catching up with your family after a year.

How are you doing with your Spanish grammar?

Nan died. Do we have time to get to the funeral? It's tomorrow. Why is it so prompt over there? I don't know.

Relationships become strained by distance and there are moments you feel you are shifting towards the margins again. Memories come to mind in a cold, practical manner, much like information acquired at school – of moments when you experienced a clash of cultures. Sometimes they happened to you, or you empathised with others.

I could tell you about nasty little kids repeating to classmates words of misplaced frustration they hear at home. Like that time in primary school when I heard a white boy say to a black boy, 'My dad's taxes paid for your new trainers'. When I became aware of racial slurs, I initially thought they were mistaken and that in my case 'Spani' must be to Spaniard what 'Paki' was to Pakistani. Words charged with offence follow no particular logic because a thing that stems from anger makes no sense.

I could tell you about the time a colleague with very little English started to cry when asked about a robbery. 'Did you see anything?' they were asking, concerned too for her own belongings, but a moment of revolt, a clash of language and previous prejudice towards her nationality resulted in her feeling interrogated rather than tended to.

I could tell you about having to put up with prejudiced comments from other women about the lingering sexism in Spain and inside my head rockets are going off and I want to pass them the mic and ask, 'How would you weigh this opinion against your tradition of changing your surname to your husband's?' I personally find changing such a defining part of your identity for a (male only) partner outdated and difficult to understand.

I can tell you stories from today such as headlines that give you the place of birth of criminals before you even get to the article. Now you're in the world of those adults the schoolyard kids used to copy when they insulted each other, remember? And they talk about things like immigrant children getting free lunch at schools because they heard someone say so. Racial insults continue to slip so easily off the tongue when charged with anger. 'But I am not racist, I just lost it,' my friend, who had been an immigrant too, explained following an argument at work. 'How would you have felt if your nationality was first on the list of insults? The very first thing that was picked up on?' If you absolutely have to, I recommended, try something along the lines of *F*** you* which spits out your rage and is pretty much nonspecific. Of course, try not to.

A clash isn't always negative. In fact, I think feeling strongly about something, even if against, can be the path to better understanding. It got your attention, after all, so it matters more to you than to a passive observer. It is necessary that we appreciate that a blend of cultures is not just about foreign people arriving and adapting to the British way of life but a conversation on both sides. There is much to be taken in from what people bring with them. We may be territorial animals when it comes to protecting our traditions, but I think you will find that when it comes to taking these traditions with us, we are more open to sharing. I am enormously lucky to have grown up in a multicultural area with a variety of places of worship and schools that celebrated all the different traditions, watching American shows featuring black families and white families, reading in more than one language and having friends who could think in different languages too.

Language is another vital component of our identity. We interpret the world according to our language. The idioms and phrases – and nowadays probably memes – that are embedded in our cultures determine how we describe and approach our everyday life. Because of this, multilingual people are likely to develop different ways of assessing information. In research, when you can't find material in one of your languages, you search in the other. Sometimes this allows you to read the same text in new ways and even obtain more information. The world as we see it is almost cubist and our heads are full of macaronic verse.

I do not recall not knowing English. It seems to me that it was always there but now I realise I spent a little while speaking with a Spanish filter before it dissolved. I also started to speak a bit of gobbledegook when I was two or three, certain that everyone else was speaking as they liked so why shouldn't I? 'She made up a language,' my mother explained at the grocery store a few months later. 'No, she's singing a Welsh song,' said the shopkeeper.

Not every immigrant has arrived at the right linguistic point of their life to acquire English in the same way. Some people might also be opposed to using their second language whenever they do not need to. For emigrated families, this can be one of the many ways of protecting their heritage. Though it may seem drastic, it makes a great deal of sense particularly for children brought up speaking a language different to yours. We can all agree nobody wants to find that they are unable to communicate with their own grandparents. A lot of the time these homes are full of language teaching on both sides. Children teach their parents better pronunciation while the parents remind them of their mother tongue.

By the time I was in school, I spoke with a thick English accent on family videos, like that of my teacher at the time. And just like that, I was bilingual. Now I often find I have to remind myself of words in Spanish if they vary drastically from their English equivalents. It is natural to be convinced that the sounds of these words I am more familiar with better describe the terms I am referring to. *Grillo* sounds too soft for a cricket and *encrespado* makes it sound like my hair is crunchy rather than frizzy!

My bilingualism allows me to hide behind my English, quietly thinking foreign thoughts and choosing to speak up against prejudice when it is brought up around me. However, the difference is that I, invisible immigrant, *can* choose. I could make up a story about a great great grandmother with Mediterranean features who passed them down to me. I could swear I was born here. I can speak like you. I get your jokes. You do not look twice at the way I dress or concern yourself with me showing my hair or not. I have no faith to argue over. I am on that margin. It is a place where colleagues' sharp eyes turn blunt when they show their xenophobia in your presence, as though to say 'Oh, we don't mean you'. They always mean another foreigner, one who dresses differently or has darker skin, a heavy accent. One they are sure is an immigrant while you were simply 'born abroad'. There is a hierarchy of nationalities when it comes to foreigners, where certain nationalities are more tolerable, not unlike the preferential treatment British people are widely known to expect when abroad. You sense that their comfortableness is with how immersed you are. You are aware of the privilege of invisibility but the world looks ugly from this position too. Masks are removed just for you and inappropriateness is permitted in your presence.

I grew up entirely in Wales and I could not say I feel half one nationality and half another. I do not believe in the math in that. I never lost my Spanish accent and my environment at home made it easy to maintain even the Andalusian expressions, and to adopt the aspirated Ss. Does that mean my children will speak English like a Welsh person thanks to me, no matter where they are? Will I take my Welshness with me? Can I? I would like to and I really think that is my decision.

To feel that we belong to a culture follows no rules. Moulded by aspects of the different customs and people we know, our minds naturally create an individuality of cultural identity within us. As non-nationals, how 'foreign' we are perceived plays a part in how foreign we feel. But we are fortunately free to be more than one thing at once. Something you *are* is not something that can be taken from you so easily. A place that has at some point been home creates an unbreakable feeling inside us that no amount of distance or rejection can change. It is important to remember that we do not belong to any culture; cultures belong to us and are shaped by us.

Everything I Will Give You

Kandace Siobhan Walker

This is a story about women and water, and it always starts with a man. He was a shepherd, he was a fisherman. He was a boy washing dishes on the Upper West Side. I was a girl who was no longer a girl. It was early summer, and I was in New York. I had taken an airplane and an overnight bus to get there. Everything was imaginable. I watched mid-century films every day in the air-conditioned guest room of my aunt's triangular redbrick in Queens and I texted boys, girls. I went to galleries and cocktail bars. I watched fireworks over the dark neighbourhoods at night. The sound was like gunfire. Sometimes it was gunfire. I was in love with the city's endless glass chambers, its dreamlike metal avenues. I walked the big park every day, after riding a bus and two trains into Manhattan. I'd wanted to swim in the reservoir at first sight. By the end of the season, my mind was made up to climb over the railing and let myself fall. Something in the water. I was heavy with grief's small stones. I knew I would sink.

Everything felt like a movie. Safe like the black-and-white films that break up daytime television. A cinematic feeling would wash over you just walking down a pretty avenue at the right time of day. The city air blew off the manmade lake in the summer. When the wind lifted, your cheeks grew cool. It was 2015 and it was the third hottest August on record. Canadian air masses normally lower the temperature, but the red line in the glass thermometer on my aunt's kitchen wall never ran below eighty.

Everywhere you went, people were sweating. We slept naked with the plug-in fans beating wind in our ears. In the sunlight, my skin glistened like I'd been swimming. I was charged by the heat. I had been walking everywhere, flying everywhere, travelling up and down the North American continent alone. Equal marriage was legalised across the country by a historic Supreme Court ruling. Next month, there would be water on Mars. The air had a sexy, desperate weight. I felt the city in my muscles, my saliva. I wanted to be changed. I wanted to be in love.

Women in love are mascots of self-sacrifice. Susan Sontag wrote about what she felt was the proportional relationship between the value of the self and that of love.[1] She warned herself against the bad habit of measuring what her love was worth by what she was willing to sacrifice.[2] Growing up a girl in the West, this was an idea I had deeply internalised. The belief that love was a self-destructive process ran deep. The evidence would be in how deeply the other person wanted to possess you, how much you were willing or able to give. At the end of my slow deconstruction, I thought I would find some great peace. I only wanted someone to take myself apart for. Marlon Brando screaming down a black-and-white street.

---

[1] Susan Sontag, *As Consciousness is Harnessed to Flesh: Diaries 1964–1980* (London: Penguin, 2013), p. 262.

[2] Sontag, p. 263.

Disney's technicolour Ariel selling her legs for a voice. Hans Christian Andersen's Little Mermaid, who must win the prince's love to earn a human soul.

In some mythical and cultural traditions, love is power – or looks like it. To be loved is to be valuable, but value does not necessarily translate to power. Stephanie Golden suggests that traditionally, love facilitates a gendered transference of power. Popular representations of romantic love fuel cultural narratives idealising self-sacrificial women, painting their sacrifice as a kind of empowerment, but self-subjugation is the opposite of power.[3]

I wanted power, I wanted love. And there is a kind of power that will seek you out, and call itself love. It will ask you to give away pieces of yourself, small enough that you don't realise until you're on dry land, confused how you wandered so far from yourself, and wondering how to get back to the water. What is more like love than relinquishing parts of yourself?

I wasn't alone, I had two sisters. Circa 1382. The historical record is not reliable. History folds back on itself until analogous events are happening simultaneously, across centuries and continents. I can't tell you who came first.

All I know is: on the beaches of a great lake in Kenya, in a small village named Nyandiwa, there was a luckless fisherman whose traps were empty every morning. And in Wales' green hills, above a small village called Myddfai, there was a lonely shepherd who watched over wild sheep and cattle grazing near a mountain lake. Each man lived by the grace of his lake. Each man met, one day, the lake's daughter.

---

[3] Stephanie Golden, *Slaying the Mermaid: Women and the Culture of Sacrifice* (Amazon, 2010), loc. 4010. Kindle.

My sisters, they must've wanted what I wanted – to be changed – to walk out of the water like that. Their shapeless figures reflecting ribbons of light, sloughing off water like skin. I don't know what they were before they broke the surface.

The woman of water is familiar. It's so easy to see how one becomes her, the path is so cleanly laid out. A Kenyan goddess.[4] A Welsh fairy.[5] William Shakespeare's Ophelia. Alfred Tennyson's Lady of Shalott. King Arthur's Lady of the Lake. The mermaids. Sirens and selkies. Rusalka. Naiads. Even Nessie. Even the brook horse is a mare.

It starts like this: she walks out of the water. Wait, no: it starts with a man without property, without position. The way he draws up an empty net, returns to barren fish traps day after day, he begins to think he is cursed. The way he talks to the animals. All you need to summon a wife from the water is a lonely and unlucky man.

We call the fisherman's lake Victoria, after an English queen. But when he pulled his future wife out of its waters, caught in the cut of his net, he would've called it Nam Lolwe. Meaning: *endless water*. It is almost a sea. It is a lake larger than Wales. Llyn y Fan Fach, the shepherd's lake, is much smaller. Its name translates to *lake of the small hill*. Names vary however, depending on who you ask. Here are two: the Kenyan fisherman was Nyamgondho, the Welsh shepherd we'll call Rhiwallon.

Rhiwallon sees her first. She isn't aware, for a moment that she's being watched. Or maybe she lets him watch her, and

<hr>

[4] Thomas Okango Atsango, *The Story of Nyamgondho* (2016), www.elimuasilia.org.

[5] W. Jenkyn Thomas, *The Welsh Fairy Book* (Mineola, NY: Dover, 2001), p. 1.

he is the one who is unaware. That is what they will say. Meanwhile, Nyamgondho drags her sister up like an anchor, an ancient, naked crone. He wants to throw her back. She must've seen the light piercing the holes in his net under the water. She swam into its grasp willingly. That's what they'll say. Had she clocked him, the skin-and-bone man who could barely catch enough to eat, let alone sell? Did she choose him?

She is nameless in Dholuo, nameless in Welsh. Sometimes she is known by a name that she did not choose. But she is always beautiful.

Take me home, says the lady to the fisherman, to the shepherd. Marry me, and I will make you rich. Some details are always the same: the lake, the beauty, her anonymity. The promise she makes, the promise he makes. What she asks of him, her fisherman, her shepherd, seems so small. But he is a man and she is a woman and we're telling a story. Something will have to break.

What the women of the water ask weighs heavy on their own shoulders, and so lightly on the men they ask it of. The lady of the lake asks Nyamgondho: never speak of where you found me. And, according to who you ask, never abuse me. The lady of the lake asks Rhiwallon: never raise your hand against me. Never touch me without kindness. It is an easy ask, an easy promise to make.

The ladies of the lakes bear fruit. Land and luxury. Cows and crops and children. The fairy of Llyn y Fan Fach has three sons. They will become doctors: the physicians of Myddfai. The oldest is named for his father. The crone of Nam Lolwe is the first wife. Her husband Nyamgondho takes two more. The second and third wives bear him children too. This is how the fisherman and the shepherd become big men. Do they know that their words are designed to break? No one realises, in the present, that these are things we will not keep.

14

The details shift depending on who's writing it down, and when. You will find Nyamgondho in some texts,[6] and in others you will find Mai, husband of Nyarmigodho.[7] Sometimes his name is Gwyn and sometimes the lady is given a name too: Nelferch.[8] Sometimes she asks him to bring her bread, but it is first too hard and then too moist. Then, sometimes, he must choose from her sisters. The lake is Llyn y Fan Fach in the Beacons or Llyn y Forwyn in the Rhondda.[9] Names are variable, but the key elements remain the same: a poor man, a body of water, a woman.

Atieno Odhiambo writes about the lady of the lake's 'translation' of Nyamgondho's poverty into prosperity.[10] It begins with a self-transformation: the fisherman pulls up an ancient woman. The next morning, she is young and beautiful. Yet her beauty serves to benefit her new husband rather than herself. The act of translation is central to mythical narratives, and what is telling is who is the beneficiary of these transformations.

Kamera and Mwakasaka note that the fisherman's marriage to the lady of the lake awards him social status in addition to wealth.[11] Even today, the Lake Victoria site is known by the name of the fisherman. Similarly, Rhiwallon's marriage gives him three sons trained in medicine, and a

---

[6] B. Onyango-Ogutu and A. A. Roscoe, *Keep My Words* (Nairobi: East African Publishing House, 1974), p. 140.

[7] Atsango.

[8] Thomas, p. 5.

[9] John Rhys, *Celtic Folklore: Welsh and Manx Volume 1* (Cambridge: University Press, 2015), p. 23.

[10] E. S. Atieno Odhiambo, 'Historicising the Deep Past in Western Kenya' in *Historical Studies and Social Change in Western Kenya,* ed. by William R. Ochieng' (Nairobi: East African Educational Publishers, 2002), p. 29.

[11] W. D. Kamera and Christon S. Mwakasaka, *The Compliment: East African Folktales* (Arusha: Eastern African Publications, 1981), p. 73.

permanent position in both the oral tradition and the historical archive – as evidenced by his presence in the medieval Welsh manuscript *Red Book of Hergest*. What does the lady of the lake gain, beyond foreshadowing? Not even a name.

The lady of the lake is neither object nor subject, but simply a narrative device – a vehicle to set the hero on his journey. Still, she is not the story's driver. Characterisations of the lady vary, although none are whole, or even flattering. At turns the cool, aloof fairy and the calculating crone, she is too mysterious to receive even sympathy. Even her plea to the fisherman in one version – 'Please don't leave me. I'm human just like yourself.'[12] – is woven into Nyamgondho's narrative, as opposed to her own. Every action she takes is an opportunity for the hero to prove himself – it is clear who we, the audience, are to empathise with, whose interiority we are to be invested in. You would be forgiven for believing this is a story about her, but you would be mistaken. Make no mistake, we are always talking about men.

Every night in New York, the sky threatened to split under its own weight, but I broke first. There was a moment when I realised that the future was unfolding itself in front of me, like a set of fingers curling away from an open palm. The nights were begging for days. I watched in the evenings for the purple clouds peeling away from the blue like skin, for the silent flashes that told me the storm was still far away.

His violence was so much like lightning that at first, I believed it was rain. I looked to the window. All I saw was myself. Just the reflection of bloodshot eyes, a split lip, two dark, bloodied nostrils, a new dullness in my skin. A girl

---

[12] Onyango-Ogutu and Roscoe, p. 140.

climbing into the shower and sitting down in the rising steam. I thought if I did the actions, I could suture the wound. The moment recedes, the sting of a slap fades. But memory is a hard thing to exorcise. Something about me had the look of a lady of water. Something in my face said: I can belong to you.

In 1846, Edgar Allan Poe claimed that a beautiful woman's death was the most poetic subject in the world.[13] It would be reductive to suggest a directly casual relationship to real experiences, but perhaps Poe's assertion reveals a cultural aesthetic that positions death as the natural state towards which femininity progresses.

In her writing, Elisabeth Bronfen asks us to interrogate the possibility of a reciprocal relationship between femininity and the process of aesthetisation, which she frames as a kind of death.[14] There is, unquestionably, an artistic tradition that reveres aesthetic representations of death as an idealised feminine state. From John William Waterhouse's *The Lady of Shalott* (1888) to Roy Lichenstein's parodic *Drowning Girl* (1963), how many images of drowning, dead or dying women hang in the halls of national galleries? Waterhouse was so moved by Tennyson's poem of the same name, first published in 1833, that he painted it in oil, two metres high. It is easy to locate the lady of the lake within this cultural imaginary. Waterhouse's Lady of Shalott floats downriver, towards her knight. She is not dead, but we know she is going to die.

The air didn't move for weeks. We walked down the streets like knives. Even when the breeze blew the uncollected trash

---

[13] Edgar Allan Poe, 'The Philosophy of Composition' in *The Poetical Works of Edgar Allan Poe* (Digital Library of America).

[14] Elisabeth Bronfen, *Over Her Dead Body: Death, Femininity and the Aesthetic* (Manchester: Manchester University Press, 1992), p. 60.

in small hurricanes down the road, it felt like we had to slice through every new day. I was old enough to know the definition of mortality, but still too immature to realise that I was not its master.

I went back to the water again and again. I walked those endless blocks like therapies. I believed I could sweat it out. I wouldn't speak it. I was like water's perfect memory: trying to return to a feeling of wholeness, of who I was.[15] Endless bodies, endless water. It was a feeling like a heavy coat draped across my shoulders. I wanted to shake it away, but could not slip free.

I wanted love to be anything. I thought love was like trees, it wasn't something invisible floating around me. It grew out of the ground like potatoes. I wanted to find a way to eat it, to pick it, to wash it and hold it clean in my hands.

Love was there for me to climb, to strip its bark away, to wear its new leaves in my hair. It was something I felt I could be, that I pictured myself as often – rising out of the water like love. And that is what it looked like, felt like, moved like, tasted like. Like love. Until it was wet iron in my mouth. Mascara pooling in the corners of my eyes. A lightness in my head. A sudden fear of movement, of sound, of breath.

Warning signs are red in the rearview: a tightness in his grip on my wrist that I mistook for want. An unwillingness to compromise that I thought was conviction. A talent for writing me out of the room, for narrating into reality a woman who lives outside of me.

I don't need to tell you, do I? He breaks the promise. The shepherd, the fisherman. It is his destiny – this is what he

---

[15] Toni Morrison, *What Moves at the Margin: Selected Nonfiction,* ed. by Carolyn C. Denard (Jackson, FL: University Press of Mississippi, 2008), p. 77.

says. It happens the way rain does, like a tree falling in a forest. No one causes it to happen, except maybe forces outside of their control. Except maybe her. Without a witness, it's easy to say it didn't happen. But there is a witness, there are two.

We're telling a story. There is no truth about it. But here's what you will hear: the fisherman and the shepherd, he is the hero. He overcomes the obstacles. He strikes his wife only by accident. He reveals her secret by mistake. He was drunk. He was innocent. Three taps on the shoulder. To ask her to move when she is still, to ask why she is crying at a christening, to ask why she is laughing at a funeral.

Here is how the myth plays out: he breaks the promise the way wind breaks the surface of the lake. She is wise, but cruel. He is just a man. There is almost a symmetry of violence. Any confession accompanied by a caveat. We can't, however, pathologise men of myth. They are not real men. But we know real men. We can draw out patterns, begin to trace the contours of a mirror image.

In the myth, the shepherd and the fisherman are absolved of fault. Their rise to a position of power provokes a sense of complete control. He never believes that she will leave him beached, with only water and a reflection. We see what was always there: he believes himself above her. If not god, then its hand.

In Rhys' *Folklore*[16] and in Glanffrwd's *Llanwynno*,[17] the lady sings as she drives the cows and the crops and the children back into the water:

---

[16] Rhys, p. 23.

[17] William Thomas, *Llanwynno Glanffrwd,* ed. by Henry Lewis (Cardiff: Gwasg Prifysgol Cmyru, 1949), p. 157.

Bwla! Bwla! Saif yn flaena'.
Tair bryncethin, tair cyffredin,
tair caseg ddu draw yn yr eithin,
deuwch i gyd i lys y brenin.

Bull! Bull! Stand thou foremost.
Three dark hills, three common,
three black mares in the gorse,
come now to the king's court.[18]

In a Kenyan retelling, the lady doesn't sing but her refrain is nonetheless lyrical: 'All that belongs to Nyamgondho, come out'.[19] The sheaths of corn uproot themselves in the field, green stalks flying over the heads of lowing cattle, the braying mare, the sweet potatoes rolling down the bank. All that belongs to you, come out. Everything I have given you, come out.

Water and resistance are synonymous. Across millennia and thousands of miles, there are realities we can't outrun. Even in the stories we tell. There are only words and promises we can keep. It is the water that births her, it's the water that takes her back. Water returning to where it was, water coming back to itself.

In both its Welsh and Kenyan contexts, the function of the myth remains the same, to warn against cruelty. Yet violence is the myth's foundation, embedded into its structure. It wears the mask of a morality tale, but the lady of the lake

---

[18] *N.B.: This verse is a condensed amalgam of the lines reported in Rhys'* Folklore *and Glanffrwd's* Llanwynno.

[19] Asenath Odaga, *Thu Thinda: Stories from Kenya* (Nairobi: Uzima Press, 1980), p. 11.

myth aestheticises femininity into a state of powerlessness. We, the audience, are invited to watch her drown. It is less for our education than our entertainment. What we mythologise is a reflection of what we value, or what we don't.

Her death simultaneously martyrs the hero, rendering him sympathetic, and gives his downfall a sense of justice, albeit misplaced. The shepherd becomes a widower. The fisherman, in his despair, ossifies into a tree on the banks of the lake whose spirit he wed and broke. Both shepherd and fisherman are returned to the condition in which we first found them: men without.

A man does wrong and he is punished. Or, a woman is wronged and punishes herself. Or, it isn't a punishment. Or, she returns somewhere she thought she couldn't get back to. Or, she takes what's hers. Or, she comes home to herself.

Here's what happened: I climbed the railing and slid into the water. I called out to everything I had given him – the summer, the evenings, the trains we'd ridden to the end of the line. Everything I would have given him – the cows, crops. All of it plummeted with me. All that belonged to him, come out.

A crowd of onlookers grew, waited for me to resurface. Watched the bubbles subside. Someone called an ambulance, a team of divers, but they couldn't find me. I was gone.

Here's what didn't happen: I didn't board an international flight with a lighter suitcase. I didn't have trouble sleeping for weeks, months. I didn't shrink away whenever someone reached out to touch me. I didn't go looking for fear in the shape of men. I didn't spend my last day in New York resting my elbows on the metal rail, letting it burn my skin, looking out over the small, manmade lake.

It was summer in New York. I was waiting for rain, and for something like love. I can't remember what I was before I broke the surface. All I know now is: I have a name.

Look At Me

Kate Cleaver

'The neighbour says that he hasn't seen a bike like this in years,' my fiancé and life-partner says. I smile. I know that it is an odd bike for the modern age. There aren't many trikes on the road, not the type that have massive baskets at the back and sit-up-and-beg handlebars. Think about a child's trike and then grow it to adult size. Mine is grey and named Trinity. She (yes, she is a she) is something I have thought about getting – but it was only recently that I took the plunge. You see, in order to get on a trike I have to admit there is a problem. There are a number of problems... Oh, and I have to hold my hands up and say I will look like a loon using the trike. It isn't the kind of bike that makes you look sophisticated; it is more of a 'poke-fun-at' machine. But to feel the wind through my hair and to be out in the sun is worth it.

I got my first trike when my parents realised there was an issue. We were living in an ex-council semi in Staffordshire and the garden was a decent size. For reasons I am uncertain about, I didn't decide that I needed a bike until my brother asked for one. So, my parents got us both one. Matt was placed on his and five minutes later, he was pedalling with no problem. Five minutes after that he had hit a tree. It took time for him to get the whole braking thing, but he was upright and riding. Stabilisers-to-bike was a quick and easy lesson.

My turn...

This did not go well. I fell. A lot. It was almost impossible and resulted in my dad picking up a trike frame from the tip on a trip to get rid of garden waste. It was heavy, but my stabilisers were bent out of shape and could no longer support me. The trike meant that I was able to fly along the pavement, perhaps not at the same speed as the other kids, but I was there, at the back.

At the back...

That is pretty much where I have been most of my life. It has always been a physical and mental thing. Firstly, I'm not white and as a kid I was much darker than I am now. Secondly, I was always mentally one step away from my peers and my younger brother's peers. Being not white in Staffordshire in the 1980s was a bit shit, to put it mildly. I could tell you the tales that my parents have passed on but perhaps the best to tell is mine. I hit puberty stupidly early; I was only 11, and it came with more pain than I had ever thought possible. When I was 'on' I would sit and rock. They didn't allow kids to carry medication and I felt it impossible to go against the rules, so I would rock. Teachers noticed, students noticed. They thought I was in trouble. So, they called in the 'experts'. Social services turned up and said – she isn't white.

I remember being taken from the playground. It was hot and I had been turning circles in the sun. I was a strange kid and the simple repetitive behaviour made me feel calmer.

'Katherine," the teacher called. I went over and was taken to a dark room. I remember the shock my skin felt from moving into such a cold environment. My skin immediately prickled up and became full of goosebumps. The room was the nurse's station, but it had been stripped. All that was left was a lamp, two chairs and a table. The lamp was the only form of lighting on and it was a harsh, nasty glare. I was told to sit in the furthest seat. How anyone could look at that set-up and think it was a good thing for a child, I have no idea. But it got past the head, deputy and a variety of staff and teachers. A slightly bald man walked in and sat down. He had a file with him, and my name was on the front.

'Hello, Katherine.'

I could tell you what was said but I'm now thirty-two years older and it has become a blur. I do remember what it was about: I'm mixed race and therefore open to more abuse than a white kid. Those were the statistics he had. That is what he believed and that is what he set out to prove. I missed lunch and afternoon break that day. They gave me a drink of water. They made me stay in that one seat, cold, and with only that lamp. And they asked me over and over whether my father was beating me. Over and over. The whole time he stared at me. I couldn't meet anyone's eyes before this, but after it was hopeless. All I wanted to yell was, don't look at me.

Never look at me.

My mum found out and she stormed into the school. She is a formidable further education teacher and back then, she used to wear these batwing capes that would billow out behind her. She swooped into that school and screamed at everyone. I was rescued. But I learnt that you don't make waves. If people looked at you then bad shit happened. As an afternote, I ought to say that the gentleman in question gained the highest grade possible in Staffordshire's social services, which included a lot of public speaking. My mum made it her mission to be at as many as she physically could.

She heckled him mercilessly, so much so that I believe he developed a nervous twitch when he saw her. Me? I never did anything, but I would love to sit the boy he had been in a cold room without a jumper and only a glass of water and repeat the same question over and over for six hours and see if he came out 'okay'.

I wasn't okay, but then I hadn't been before I stepped into that room. I was a little odd. My aunt once asked my mum, many years later, if I was alright… mentally. She stretched out that word and mouthed it rather than spoke it. It was a valid question. I was living with her at the time while I worked at a conservation place nearby. I brought knitting. I didn't go out. I didn't make friends. I was alone most of the time; both in and out of work. My mum's reply was a simple no. That shocked me a bit. Was I wrong? Different, yes, I'd admit to that. I had got so good at hiding though… So very good. I was even hiding from myself.

Nobody ever looked at me.

I was 38 when I finally found out that I was autistic, dyspraxic and dyslexic. I was doing my master's and struggling. Once I found out, it all made sense. I remember sitting in the office that was always hot and smelled slightly dusty despite being a new build. The combination made me remember a time of heat and dust. Not the type of sun we get in Wales, but a life-sucking sun that has parched the ground too much. Suddenly I was back in Majorca, my toes dug into almost white sand. Not the heavy beat of bass and the false lights of a rave, but the other side of the island. The part that was open to the elements and the locals. Where you must be able to speak some Spanish and the only tourists were hardened Germans in hot-footed socked sandals. I was there with my undergraduate degree.

I didn't know what was wrong with me then. I was good

26

at what I did but I was hiding. I was out drawing plants; it was a joint degree in art and biology.

'You never look at people,' she said. 'Why?'

My companion was older than me. I found it easier to get on with those on the periphery of society, and she sat happily on the weird shoulder of life.

'I don't know,' I said.

'We need to fix that.'

I looked at a tree just behind her and off to the left. 'I guess.'

'It is no way to live.'

From that day on when she spoke to me, she told me to look at her. If the internet had been what it is today, I would probably have been one of those people, up to that point, that would have had the best Instagram account around. My life would have seemed perfect. I know because at the time, I did it all with a camera. I have books and books of photos and my life looks perfect. It wasn't. All the friends that are there… I'm not sure I knew any of them.

Look at me.

If you have been taught to hide all your life, how do you do it?

I never told her that it hurt. An actual physical pain. Don't think I have ever admitted that… Slowly I got used to the pain. I started to look at her ear.

'My eyes,' she would say.

I would try but that hurt the worst. I found that, if I focused, I could look at her nose.

'That's it!' she exclaimed.

It wasn't but it was the best I could do.

Look at me.

It became her catchphrase. The thing that she said all the time. Look at sodding me. Some of me hated it and a tiny part said that I needed to learn this. So, I persevered. After a year, she stopped saying it. After another month or so, I realised I was looking at her eyes, and they were brown. I wish she was still here because she would see that it doesn't show. Not anymore. My autism is well-hidden, tucked away inside.

Sometimes I still don't understand everything. There is always more to learn about social interaction, but what was in the past plain mimicry is now understanding. At school I would laugh at the jokes or, to my shame, at others because I wanted to fit in. I had to hide.

No one look at me. I'm not important. I'm not really here.

Back then, at school I was described as frigid or aloof. That I looked down on people. I once remember watching everyone look at each other's marks for the year. I held mine in a loose hand, the small green book that listed everything you had succeeded and failed in. Back and forth those books went. No one reached for mine and no one handed me theirs. I waited. 'Can I see?' I want to say that my voice was strong and confident, but it wasn't. I stared at the floor and my voice was barely above a whisper. One girl handed me her book and took mine.

'Straight A's,' she said. 'Boring.'

And that was it. My book was left on the side and everyone filed out. I had tried to be social. It hadn't worked, and I was confused as to what I'd done wrong. Surely As were good. I went home. I gave my mum the book and she nodded, said well done and told me I needed to walk the dog. I had more of a social life with my pet than I did with any person. Tabby – yes, I'm aware it is a cat's name – was my best friend. She didn't care that I would obsess about stuff. That I could read a book and get so engrossed that it took over my life. Of course, the whole fact that I was reading was a bit of a miracle. I'd hit my eleventh year when my mum had been called into school. Mum has an old wound on her leg, so she slightly drags it. It's tiny but I could hear her as soon as she entered the school. She came charging down the corridor and straight into the headmaster's room. I've always wished I knew what was said, but she came out and we left. It had been the last day of school before the summer holidays.

'You are going to learn how to read,' she said. 'And ride a bike.'

That was my dream. To ride a bike. My trike had become too eye-catching. People stared and I didn't want that. We had been trying to get me to balance for months, but it wasn't happening. I looked back at the door to the headmaster's office and I saw him stood there. He was looking at me with such pity. It wasn't until I was an adult that I learnt that they had been about to move me into a special school, but mum had argued for one more summer. They gave it to her. We walked out of that school with one task – I had to read.

Everyday my mum would push that bike, running back and forth. I was almost the height I am now, so my bike was for an adult despite me being only ten. Back and forth on the grass outside the house. Everyone saw.

'But they see,' I whined.

'Shut up and get on,' she said. I'd fallen again and was bleeding from a knee.

'But…'

She just looked on. I got on and tried again. And again. So many times. The only thing going through my head was the fact that people could see. I was on this bike, on the green and we were doing something that yelled: LOOK AT ME. I was mortified.

Sometimes I wonder if it was that mortification that motivated me, as by the end of the summer, I could almost ride. I never got any better. I was fine going straight but bends caused a problem. I fell. A lot. Of course, now I know that research has shown that by mixing balance and learning a new skill like writing, the dyslexic brain creates new pathways. Think of the brain as a computer; a dyslexic is wired differently to others, but it can be re-routed. That is what happened that summer. With every turn of the pedal, I got closer to learning to read. I didn't know but my drive for people to not stare opened the world of words to me. One day, I picked up a copy of *The Hundred and One Dalmations* by Dodie Smith and I just read it. No hesitation. That night, I wobbled on my bike across the green. I was riding.

'We need to go riding,' my love said last year.

'Bikes?'

'Yes,' he said.

I saw the crashes from the past and looked down at my too-heavy 40-year-old body and shook my head. 'I can't.'

What I meant to say was that I don't bounce like I used to. He frowned and said it would take time. Then we tried. I cried and shook. We got a trike and now I can cycle where I want. No bouncing needed. Oddly, I don't worry about the looks. You see, my head no longer worries about that. I know what is wrong with me and rather than fight it, I decided the best thing was to embrace it. I guess it helps that I was thirty-eight when everything was found out. I was starting to question my sanity and was heartily fed up of hiding. Don't look at me had become tiresome.

I was working from home and apart from a commute to my shed, that took about twenty steps, I didn't get out at all. Don't get me wrong, when I started it was exactly what I needed, but as time wore on, I learnt more and more coping strategies. Looking people in the eye stopped hurting and became easy; writing became easier the more I did it; drawing allowed me to express everything; I no longer panicked in crowds because I'd plan a way out. And of course, the smart phone, that tiny invention. A mobile PA that would tell me where I had to be and how to get there. I didn't have to hold time and places in my head because it was right there, on the phone. I was ready to fly but I knew there was something wrong.

A few tests later, as part of an investigation when I was doing my masters, I had the answers. I wasn't mad or broken, I was just different. That has been the hardest thing. To realise I'm not some broken person, not something that ought to be thrown away. I can stand up and be me; I'm just odder than others. Most people don't realise I'm neurodivergent. It's an invisible thing and one I am glad is. I can be seen as a creative and a little strange, but no one points and says, "Look at her." Not anymore.

I'm getting married this year. Shocker. Who'd ever have thought I'd get married? The girl who couldn't meet your eyes and was unable to navigate a social conversation. But I am and on that day, one thing will be going through my head.

Look at me.

I don't need to think of myself as needing to say sorry for living. I make a difference and I think it is a good one. I suppose you could say I live inside my own carefully constructed shell. Perhaps once it was a shell or rather the skin I wished I had. Now though, I inhabit it to its full extent. I am unusual and life is a challenge, but I love it.

Don't you see?

Look at me.

Language as Water

Grug Muse

I

dilute
i forget the arabic word for *economy*
i forget the english word for لسع forget
the arabic word for *incense* & the english
word for نيكسم arabic word for *sandwich*
english for واللہ & ةيلديص & معطم
/ stupid girl, atlantic got your tongue/
         – Safia Elhillo, *The January Children*[20]

In her poem 'To make use of water' Safia Elhillo talks of when
her English gives out to Arabic, and English creeps into her
Arabic as dilution. She forgets words in both languages and
finds herself swimming in the space between them. A
member of the Sudanese-American diaspora, she chastises
herself: 'stupid girl, Atlantic got your tongue'. It's a familiar
feeling for anyone who has more than one language

---

[20] Elhillo, Safia, *The January children* (Lincoln, NE: University of Nebraska Press, 2017).

competing in their heads, patching the holes in one with bits of the other, always impure, bastardised – diluted.

In Safia's poem, language becomes water, and water is fluid and dangerous, a substance where one can swim or drown. To imagine language as water is to give it the quality of both the bridge and the border. It can act as a substance through which things move, or objects are carried; equally it can seep into materials and change them, ruin or destroy them. It can sit still, in a pool, or it can rush and crash and destroy. We are 70% formed of water and can drown in a teacup of it. It has been a marine highway, connecting people and cultures; transporting slaves and war machines. It hides sea monsters, it waters our gardens.

Like language, water is changeable and our relationship to it depends on whether we are drinking from it, sailing on it or drowning in it. Both are inconsistent, their forms ever changing.

In a recent S4C documentary, a man is interviewing a Spanish fascist. *'Ojalá'* the fascist says. *'Ojalá*, soon we will get rid of the Muslims from Spain'. *Ojalá*, meaning 'God willing', from the Arabic *'Law shaa Allah'* ('and God wished') – medieval Arabic seeping into Spanish. Language like liquid.

During the war in Bosnia in the 1990s, Welsh is used by the Royal Welch Fusiliers to encrypt radio communications and hide messages from interference. Language as moat.

'Na, dim diolch,' I say to a man trying to sell me a wristband on the Bangor High Street.

'Why don't you fucking speak English like everyone else you fucking twat?'

Language as ice, cracking and breaking under you, sending you crashing into the water below.

II

In the dystopian world of *Y Dydd Olaf* [*The Last Day*] (1976), robots have taken over. Marc is doomed, but his thoughts and memories are preserved for future generations from the insidious robot take over by his ability to speak Welsh, a language so insignificant that the robots have deleted all trace of it from their hard drives in order to save space. In the book, Marc wages a guerrilla-linguistic war of resistance, a lonely campaign for his own sanity, one man against the hegemonic power of a monocultural majority.

> *Mae Nhw wedi anghofio un peth: wedi anghofio fod rhan o'r rhaglen gyfieithu is-ieithoedd ar gyfer yr Uchel Gyfrifydd wedi'i dileu ers amser. Ac heb wybod fy mod i'n gwybod hynny!*
>
> *Yr hollwybodus ei hun, yn methu deall fy iaith fach i!*
>
> *Fe â'r dyddiadur hwn drwy'i grombil electronaidd heb roi cam-dreuliad iddo! Fydd o'n darganfod dim yn hwn sy'n waharddedig – oherwydd nid yw'n deall yr un gair o'r iaith fach ddibwys hon! Ac fe fydd popeth – y gwaharddedig a'r diwaharddedig – yn cael eu micro-ffilmio a'u storio'n ddianaf yn y cof electronaidd.*

['They have forgotten one thing: have forgotten that part of the sub-language translation programme for the High Computer has been deleted. And they don't know that I know!

The All-knowing himself – unable to understand my little language!

This diary will pass through his electronic depths without giving him indigestion! He will discover nothing which is forbidden in it – because he doesn't

34

understand a word of this little worthless language! And so everything – the forbidden and un-forbidden – will be micro-filmed and stored, unharmed, in the electronic memory.']²¹

Y Dydd Olaf is a modern classic. Out of print, it's available only through the generosity of the copyright holders as a free online download. Printed off, words disappearing off the top margin, held together by a crinkled plastic wallet, it seems like a facsimile of the document the text purports to be. The unofficial account of the end of humanity, written in a language considered too insignificant to be a threat. Dead and unimportant, it survives as an accident, in spite of itself.

The book is part of a wider body of dystopian, utopian and sci-fi literature obsessed with the Welsh language, and its extinction or survival. *Wythnos yng Nghymru fydd*²² [*A week in the Wales to be*] (1957) by Islwyn Ffowc Elis is typical of most postures assumed in these books, imagining both a utopian, fully bilingual Wales, where English and Welsh are truly equal, as well as a dystopian Wales where not only has the Welsh language died, but so has basic human decency. *Y Dydd Olaf* is different in that it takes the existentialist panic head on, turns the languages' relative obscurity into a strength, a defence against monocultural hegemony. Forty years later, as computers and phones are increasingly listening into all our conversations, speaking a language the computer doesn't understand, or at least is not being paid to provide targeted advertising to its speakers, feels increasingly like a blessing.

Despite the defiant tone of the book however, Marc is still a tragic figure, an isolated speaker of his language. By writing

---

²¹ Owain, Owain, *Y Dydd Olaf* (Llandysul: Gwasg Gomer, 1976).

²² Elis, Islwyn Ffowc, *Wythnos yng Nghymru Fydd* (Cymru: Plaid Cymru, 1957).

in Welsh he is evading the censorship of the robots, but equally, he is writing unsure whether anyone will ever be able to understand or decipher his document. He is speaking into an abyss.

Since the 1980s marine scientists have followed a similar creature, something calling out in a private language, waiting seemingly in vain for someone to understand, and answer. It is the sound made by an unidentified whale, whose calls resonate at 52hz, much higher than the blue whale's 10-39 hz call, and the fin whale's 20hz. It has never been seen, only heard. Like a neighbour climbing their stairs next door, scientists have listened to the 52hz whale move between the Aleutians in northern Alaska, down to the coast of California, swimming distances of 30 to 70 km a day for 30 years. Like Marc's language in *Y Dydd Olaf*, the whale is considered somehow defective. Scientists speculate that its unique frequency is the result of a malformation, or that it is a cross between a blue and fin whale. Members of the deaf community have suggested that it may simply be deaf. It is certainly a maverick. Its path does not follow the seasonal migration patterns of other whales. It seems to prefer its own company. Or maybe it is hiding? Is ostracised? Is searching for something? It is tempting to anthropomorphise, to project human narratives onto this enigmatic creature. There is something so deeply compelling about the story of a whale that has been calling out for 30 years without ever receiving an answer.

Unlike the whale, however, Marc is bilingual. His isolation is selective. As an eight-year-old, I was not yet fully bilingual, and my father's family, all American, were all monolingual English speakers. At my grandparent's house in Massachusetts, I sit at the top of the stairs, hidden in the shadows of the dark attic, arms folded over my knees. My plan had been to hide up here until the adults in the parlour below had forgotten about me, before jumping down to surprise them. But now I have become engrossed, eavesdropping on the conversations going on below and have forgotten all about scaring them.

My American cousins cannot understand me talk. I can barely understand them either. When my grandmother takes me and my siblings onto her lap to read us story books, as she has done with all my other cousins, we quickly get bored of listening to stories in a language we do not understand. We become restless, badly behaved. My older cousins tease me when the sentences I am trying to form get tangled in my mouth and come out misshapen or broken. I grow frustrated, lash out. I do not understand and am not able to make myself understood. And now they are sat downstairs, talking in exasperated voices about what a badly-behaved child I am, how me and my siblings don't know how to behave, how we aren't like the other children who love their grandmothers' stories and sit listening quietly.

I stay up on top of the stairs till they finish their conversations and have dispersed around the house and garden. I wait till my face has lost all its blotchiness before creeping back downstairs. My English improves. I don't believe a whale would choose monolingualism.

III

I cross the River Taff daily on my way from Grangetown, where I currently live, into town. Just below the Millennium Stadium, two bridges cross the river, one for the trains and the other for cars and pedestrians. The Taff has been diverted, it is now flowing through an artificial culvert, further west than it used to flow in 1830. The water is green and murky. When the rain has been heavy the river swells, a frothing brown, and you can stand on the bridge and watch debris sweep by from upstream – bits of plastic, branches and pieces of wood, anything that floats. Once, when the water was still enough for the silt to sink back to the bottom, I saw a turtle paddling in the shallow water.

I once biked up the Taf, through Pontypridd, Abercynon and Treharris, Aberfan and Abercanaid to Merthyr, where Taf Fawr and Taf Fechan join. From there, I followed the Fechan up into the Brecon Beacons, into the Pontsticill reservoir, climbing higher and higher, watching it disappear into the hills, to the drained reservoir at Neuadd then up to its source, on the southern slope of Pen y Fan.

At its mouth, the river now mixes with the Ely and sea water to form the tidal lake around which the new Cardiff Bay is being developed; expensive apartments and exciting sporting facilities, the administrative and governmental buildings of the New Wales, filming studios, fashionable cafés and restaurants.

A few weeks after my bike ride up the Taf I am getting my bike fixed in Cardiff, in a small bike shop near the river. The man asks for my phone number, to let me know when he will be done, and I have to repeat it twice, because he says he does not understand my accent.

He asks for my name, and again I am asked to repeat it twice, and then spell it out.

'Haven't heard that name before,' he says.

'It's Welsh,' I reply.

'Well so am I,' he says, suddenly defensive. I didn't say you weren't, I think, yet here we are, both suddenly foreign, both swirling in the waters of the Taf estuary.

There is no word in English that conveys the difference between *Cymraeg* and *Cymreig*. Both meanings – *Cymraeg*, meaning something pertaining to the Welsh language, and

Cymreig, something pertaining to Wales – are squeezed into the English word 'Welsh'. A language is not a country. It's a universe, and when you shift between one and the other the nature of reality shifts slightly with you. When llynnoedd change into lakes, nentydd into streams their nature changes slightly also.

IV

> *'Fesul tŷ, nid fesul ton*
> *y daw'r môr dros dir Meirion'*
> [The sea will swallow Meirion
> not wave by wave, but house by house']²³

Metaphors of drowning are often used to describe the situation of the Welsh language. Inundations, floods, and sweeping tides are invoked to describe the sweeping away of the Welsh language. It is repeated in songs and poems and paintings and books. And nowhere is this metaphor more poignantly made true than in the actual drowning of Cwm Celyn in 1965. A wholly Welsh-speaking village, its residents were relocated in order for the valley to be turned into a reservoir, to supply the city of Liverpool with water. People still, on occasion, pull in at the side of the road to piss into the lake.

The image of a watery-ghost village, a submarine grave, caught the popular imagination, sparking protests at the time, nationalist politicians swept down onto the small village, and inspired young people to try their hands at amateur incendiary device construction²⁴ and vandalism. The impact

---

²³ Owen, Stad Gerallt Lloyd, *Cilmeri a cherddi eraill* (Caernarfon: Gwasg Gwynedd, 1991).

²⁴ In 1963, during the construction of the dam, Emyr Llywelyn, Owain Williams and John Albert Jones were sentenced for placing a bomb in an electrical transmitter at the site of the dam.

of the drowning of Capel Celyn, to create the Tryweryn reservoir, far outlasted the 60s. It inspired pop songs, a wealth of mediocre poetry, and a sustained graffiti campaign.[25]

The summer of 2018, and a heatwave drives the water levels of the Tryweryn reservoir to the lowest it's been for many years. The Arenig behind it is a barren grey of dried grass. After weeks of sun, mist has descended, but the level of the reservoir continues to drop as the rate of water consumption by the city of Liverpool outstrips the level of rainfall.

Travelling from Bala to Caernarfon, I pass by the reservoir and can't resist pulling into one of the laybys to have a look. I pull in by the memorial chapel at the western end of the reservoir, where the old bridge used to cross the Tryweryn River above the village. It begins to rain heavily as I creep through the trees at the shore, coming down to the rocky beach. Below me the exposed shoreline has revealed some of the remains of the village. A thick layer of silt and mud covers the whole area, cracked by the heat. Barren, like the moon, the shapes give way to meaning and form a map of the former village. The roots of hedges survive, marking the borders of fields. The compressed earth of roads and paths have survived the erosion of lake water and have become raised tracks. The remains of walls are also visible, as is the riverbed that the Tryweryn is now again trickling down. Further up the shore, someone has found the sign for one of the farms, still intact, a signpost for a place abandoned for fifty years.

I walk further down, deeper into the lake bed. It is thrilling to walk on what is usually submerged, and I am not the only one here. I find pieces of blue china, half submerged in the water, pick them up, wipe them clean and put them in my

---

[25] Google 'Cofiwch Dryweryn'. I dare you.

pocket. Even in the rain, people appear from the trees up along the former shoreline, venture onto the muddy lakebed, poke in the mud. Parents bring children to see the drowned village. It has become a perverse pilgrimage. This, they seem to say, this is our existential fear made tangible. It's a wound, and we don't want to poke it as much as to climb into it and curl up in it.

I have now ventured too far down. Although the surface of the mud seems dry, the water table is not as far below as it seems and under the surface crust the mud is deep, and soft, and I begin to sink. I turn back to the shore, try to make my way back, but I am sinking. My shoes are getting stuck, filling with mud so I take them off and carry them. I am sinking up to my knees in soft, claylike mud, and for a moment I think I might drown, get pulled into the depth of the lake. But of course, I don't. I clamber, using my hands, mud now in my hair and on my face, and climb out of the lake, back into my car, where I drive home in my underwear, wrapped in an old blanket, hair dripping fat droplets onto the seat.

Dear O

Josh Weeks

5th January 2019

Dear O,

I've been thinking about you a lot lately. Not because I'm bored or defeatist or nostalgic. I'm not dying – as far as I know – and even if I was I doubt there'd be much you could do to me. No, this is something different. This is no strings attached. I have tried, in my way, to be free.

*

Living with OCD is like making a deal with the devil. Short-term euphoria. Long-term misery. It's the scab you *need* to pick at, knowing full well it'll leave a scar. It's that dickhead of a friend you can never quite bring yourself to hate.

Picture the scenario: the city-centre at rush hour. It's a Friday night, chucking it down, and everyone's desperate to get home and start their weekend. I'm no different – I've just finished a 40-hour week at Waterstones, and I've got a night out with friends planned that I've been looking forward to since Monday.

I've been waiting on the traffic lights for a minute or so. I can feel my heart-rate beating faster. And faster. The bodies have been multiplying since I emerged from the Hayes, and now they've joined forces in an ephemeral protest against the travails of the working week. The lights turn to red; the little man flashes green. The crowd surges forward in a single, giant mass. I take the deepest of breaths. I step out into the road.

The onslaught of worn-out sales assistants in sensible shoes sends puddle-water splashing across my shins. Drivers are honking their horns for no apparent reason. My body is so tense I'm struggling to move. Each tiny step feels like I'm fighting the laws of a vertical gravity – an invisible force field between me and the train station. I can't afford to miss the 18:08 to Severn Tunnel Junction.

Danger. A woman. She's carrying a baby. It's strapped to her front in a baby sling, and her partner is holding an umbrella to protect them from the rain. They were a part of the crowd but they've somehow peeled away – their contours sharpen as everything around them dissolves. My heart is beating so fast I can barely breathe. The baby can't be more than a few weeks old.

Then the whispering begins. *You're going to hurt the baby.* The harder I try to block it out the louder it gets. *You're going to push the woman… the baby's going to fall and die.* By this point I've given up on moving altogether; I'm standing dead still in the middle of the crossing, hoping to God I can make it through this moment.

The woman is approaching. *BABY.* She's getting closer and closer. *KILLER.* The baby's crying rises above the car horns. *BABY KILLER, BABY KILLER!*

As the woman passes by me, I feel a nerve in my right arm twitch…

The next thing I know it's just me in the road, a parade of angry drivers with their heads out the window screaming at me to move. I run to the pavement and wait an agonising minute for the lights to go red again. When the cars have stopped, I hurry back out into the road and search the floor for evidence of a crime.

I do this at least four times. Red light, check. Green light, wait. I don't know what it is I'm looking for exactly, but I need to be certain that the twitch in my right arm wasn't an intentional movement. When I've finally come to terms with the fact that there's nothing in the road that's going to give me this reassurance, I head to the nearest coffee shop, lock myself in the toilet, and unlock my phone.

I'm in there for fifteen minutes or so, lost in a Google black-hole that starts with *define attempted murder* and comes to a reluctant end with *is psychosis a valid legal defense?* Nothing I look at gives me relief. Even if there were a blog or webpage that could quell my fear, it wouldn't take me long to question its validity. When I finally come out there's a restless queue of people waiting for the toilet. I have no idea if it's the anxiety or the shame, but as I pass them by, I swear they're staring at me in disgust.

By the time I get home it's 10pm – I'm still unsure if I'm a dangerous criminal or not – and all hopes of a fun Friday night have well and truly vanished. I don't touch the Indian takeaway that's been sitting in the microwave for three hours, and the only activity I can muster the energy for is to fall back onto the sofa and flick through the TV guide. When I see that *The Shining* is about to start, I wonder whether a corner of the evening could still be salvaged; I've probably seen it a dozen times, but Kubrick's my saving grace.

After less than five minutes I turn it off and go to bed. I'm convinced I'm Jack Torrance with a shaved head and a Welsh accent.

6th January 2019

Dear O,

Do you remember when we first met? If I'm honest, I don't know if I can. The image in my head has been coloured with strange light; the sun filtered through various shades of red and indigo. I walk through an archway and I'm hit by the smell – a pungent incense that could wake the dead, or at least bring the dying back from the brink. I make my way between benches and kneeling figures. All the wealth in the world is contained in the golden chalice sitting on the altar. The man in front of me, who barely knows my name, leads me into a corner that has been closed off expressly for the occasion. He says his piece and it's my time to respond. 'I once slammed a door when I was angry at my parents…' And that's when I get a glimpse of you – not emerging from the shadows; not reflected in the eyes set upon me, a mixture of self-importance and pity. You're just this incorporeal presence filling the space behind my eyes. Both nowhere and everywhere. Like a plague of insects, or something rotten burning. And yet, for all the putrid fear, for all the hallowed sickness swaying in my stomach, I get a sense of déjà vu more eerie than the organ playing in the background. And I mean Eyes Wide Shut*-eerie – the dance hall scene. Or better yet, faking the moon landing. I wonder whether you've actually been with me all along, and the whole scene is a Kubrick-style mind-fuck designed to give you form.*

*

There are schools of thought that just can't agree. Watson and Freud. Guardiola and Mourinho. The behaviourists believe that it's all just stimuli – the brain as *tabula rasa* that feeds on information inputs. The psychoanalysts, meanwhile, yearn for structure and commonalities. The three-tiered ego marks the proving ground of desire.

Like all reasonable laymen, I understood that I shouldn't judge either before I had tried both of their methods. After all, isn't it always the case that the answer lies somewhere in the middle?

The psychoanalyst was first. He charged £120 a session, but a pristine top hat hung on the back of his office door, and I convinced myself – by way of his carefully sculpted moustache – that he may well have been one of Sigmund's protégées.

According to him, I was firmly rooted at the sharpest point of an Oedipal triangle. I felt guilty and ashamed, and things wouldn't change until I was ready to relive whatever trauma I had repressed. We spoke about my mother: whether I dreamed about her cooking, her perfume, the feel of her fur coat. My father, he suggested, was like God or a Mafia Don. Once you've asked for help you know you're in it for the long haul.

For a month or so I didn't feel any different. Once a week my dad would pick me up from work and we'd head straight over to Bristol. Every time I heard the crunch of the gravel drive beneath the tires, my faint optimism quickly mutated into fear, and I'd prepare myself for the inevitable interview: *How was your childhood?* Happy. *How did you feel when your younger brothers were born?* Ecstatic. Scared. Like the world was shifting on its axis.

He once told me to close my eyes and imagine a special place. My phone sat on the arm of my chair, recording each stage of the ritual.

Where are you?
A beach.
Which beach?
I don't know.
Is it sunny?
It's boiling.
Are you alone?
No, there's a girl.

I followed each command to breathe in, breathe out – imagined I was on this unknown beach with this unknown girl, feeling an unknown happiness that was emptiness as well. It felt vaguely therapeutic, like screaming underwater, but I couldn't help but think it was evasion over action. Because how can you find peace when it's prescribed at daily intervals? I knew full well that once I'd reached the surface O would be there waiting for me, fiercer and more determined than ever.

7th January 2019

Dear O,

You've taken too much from me, but I'm way past regretting. I'm way past fantasising about how much better things could have been.

It's not that I'm in denial about what you are and what you've done. I've replayed all the wasted moments a million times over, and I admit, it hurts to think of all the pain you caused – not just to me, but to everyone I love. It's just that I've come to realise that there are a million other moments yet to be lived, waiting for me outside the prison of my mind. I'm not willing to let those moments pass me by anymore.

I'm done with hating you, O. I'm done with trying to make you disappear. There's that cliché, 'nobody said life was easy,' but I've started to question whether it really holds weight – whether the majority of people really do want an easy life. Because I think our demons help to complete us, in a perverse kind of way; their frustrated desires set the banal ablaze, stoked by reserves of strength we never knew we had.

We're still in January, and the sky is the colour of Dorothy's Kansas. But for some strange reason, I can't seem to take my eyes off it.

*

If the 'talking about it' cure was the psychoanalyst's preferred method of treatment, my GP had neither the time nor the expertise to venture beyond the prescription pad.

Antidepressants might help…

Are there any side effects?

A few – but nothing too serious.

He certainly didn't tell me about what I've come to call the 'mirror stage' (not to be confused with its Lacanian equivalent) where the hours spent staring at my reflection seemed a little unhealthy. I'd arrive at work for the beginning of my shift, but after five minutes on the shop floor I'd slink away to the employee bathroom for as long as I could without being missed.

When the serotonin first started kicking in, looking at myself in the mirror was like an out-of-body experience. The sun shining through the window was nothing short of a spotlight, and were it not for the sound of my boss's voice on the other side of the toilet door, drifting away into the stratosphere might have seemed like a genuine possibility. I'd just stand there watching myself as if I needed visible proof that what I was feeling was real: voided, weightless, lacking in physical substance. It was an absence in the pit of my stomach where there used to be butterflies or moths or whatever the fuck made me feel like vomiting every time the ten o'clock news came on.

At home things had changed as well. I used to struggle to get to sleep, but now I was sleeping like a baby pumped with breast milk and Calpol. I knew that the pills might make me tired, but I wasn't ready for the perpetual siesta that hit me in those first few weeks, when the mirror and the sunlight were my favourite forms of recreation. As for meals, movies, coffee breaks – they seemed to dissolve the very moment they came into being. Even being caked in mud on the football field on a Saturday morning felt like walking on the moon.

But suffice to say, Prozac time – like all time – is relative, and it didn't take long for my trips to the employee bathroom to begin to dwindle. As far as I could see there were three possibilities: 1. my tolerance had increased, 2. they were filling my prescription box with sugar capsules, or 3. I was getting worse. Another trip to the doctor's surgery landed me firmly in camp 3. When the GP upped my dosage (three tablets, habitually downed with one gulp of water at breakfast) the sense of weightlessness vanished completely. Catching a glimpse of the daily headlines was as terrifying as it had always been, and the days dragged like an invisible hand was meddling with the clock. Even football was beginning to lose its novelty, with injuries and waterlogged pitches coinciding with what seemed to be the end of my Prozac honeymoon period.

My Mum dragged me along to the surgery for a third time. She said that she was worried about me – that the pills had stopped working; that she'd told me time and time again that it was all in my head but it was like talking to a brick wall. She said that she didn't know what to do.

'We could try him on Valium...' the doctor said to my Mum. When he leaned in to talk to me, I noticed that his breath smelt like menthol cigarettes.

He told me it would calm me down and give me time to think. When he said it might make me sleepy, I almost burst out laughing.

'They're great for the short-term, but I wouldn't recommend you taking them for longer than a few days —'

'Then what *do* you recommend?' I asked, unable to hide my desperation.

For a moment he looked at me like I was an ungrateful little shit. Then he asked for my weekly schedule. Then he put my name on a waiting list.

I can't remember what I was expecting from that trip to the surgery, but I do know that the second I was back in the car I was already craving a new obsession.

At home it was tears and fruitless reassurance.

'Why can't you put it behind you?' asked my mum.

'I don't know.' I whispered. 'I just can't.'

I finished my course of Valium and went back to the drawing board. I came up with the bright idea of trying to rationalise every idea that came into my head. I told myself that if I lay in bed for long enough I could study every last detail of a chosen memory, and cancel them out one by one until all the destructive possibilities were exhausted. But imagine playing chess against a part of yourself that's programmed to be unbeatable. Or boxing an opponent who gets to his feet, again and again, even after the most brutal of haymakers. I was destined to lose.

Then I got the call. *We can pencil you in for Saturday morning?* I was meant to be playing football that day, but I'd have missed my own funeral if it meant getting better.

'Great, I'll be there.'

'Arrive ten minutes early, if you could.'

When I turned to my mum and saw that she was crying, I didn't know whether it was relief or sheer exhaustion.

8th January 2019

Dear O,

I never thought I'd say this, but it's no longer just you and me. I've started telling my friends about you – I've started spitting out my deepest, darkest secrets as if they were nothing more than passing thoughts, because finally – after all this time – I realise that's exactly what they are.

Everyone I've told says you're just a bully, but I think that's a little too simplistic. You're more like a lifeguard who thinks that the whole world is drowning in the deep end, or a well-meaning confidant who asks question after question at the expense of giving comfort. Really, I mean it – I don't think you're evil. Seriously misguided, yes. But I think your intentions are good. Be that as it may, I don't really care about your motives. It's the effect you've had that matters.

Yes, we can still talk, but I won't take your words as gospel. Yes, I'll still write to you, but it certainly won't be asking for advice. Things have changed, O – I think you already know that. I'm no longer the scared little boy I used to be, and no matter what you try telling me, I've come too far to let anything you say change that. I've got my friends to help me if I find myself struggling to stay afloat. They listen, but don't judge. And the only question they ever ask is why I didn't tell them about all of this sooner.

*

Then it started… not just the recovery, but the fucking realisation! It was like watching *Full Metal Jacket* instead of Trump's inauguration, or leaving Manchester United to join the Pep revolution at City. It might sound like I'm joking, but I'm being deadly, *deadly* serious. Age-old platitudes exploding into a million moving images. Mourinho's turgid football swapped for a more fluid approach to the beautiful game.

> *I think you have OCD*
> *I'm sorry, I have what...?*
> *Pure O, to be specific – but it's best not to put a label on it.*

CBT is hard to digest. Not because it's complicated, but because it's so excruciatingly simple. During our first session together my therapist pulled out his smartphone. He began to show me a video. A snail and a hand and a stopwatch. A slimy head emerged from the shell, but when the snail began to move, the hand dropped a stone beside it. The stone hit the floor and the snail returned to hiding. The words '5 seconds' flashed across the screen.

And on and on it went. Snail. Stone. Shell. Stopwatch. For a moment I thought of *Groundhog Day* and pictured Bill Murray walking me through the basics of neurology, but my therapist had a Birmingham accent that could shatter the most stubborn of daydreams.

'Do you get it?'

'Get what?'

'You're the snail,' he said, smiling like a maniac.

I asked him to elaborate and he opened up an app.

'This is your amygdala.' He was prodding his finger towards a cartoon brain, focusing my attention on an almond-shaped structure near the centre. 'It's the animal in us all – pure instinct; fight or flight. When you sense danger an alarm goes off, and this part of your brain is screaming for you to react. The problem we have is that, in your case, the amygdala is far too overactive... every time you feel danger or anxiety, you crawl back into your comfort zone. It just so happens that *your* comfort zone takes the form of checking and ruminating – seeking reassurance.'

'But the snail kept on hiding,' I said. 'He crawled back into his shell every time the stone fell.' The therapist returned his phone to his pocket and pulled his chair closer to mine.

'You can't beat it overnight. Yes, the snail sensed danger, but with each consecutive drop, the time it took for him to come *back out* of the shell gradually decreased. If we can get you to face your fear rather than running away, the amount of time you spend ruminating will lessen significantly. The hope is to one day get you to a stage where you don't feel the need to hide at all.'

The sun was coming through the window, warming the back of my neck. On the far side of a split-second, I saw something resembling hope.

9th January 2019

Dear O,

I've met someone. Her name's Grace, and when she laughs it's like summer and honey and football under floodlights. Her favourite movie is Forrest Gump. *It's growing on me day by day.*

*

Okay, I admit it. I may have gotten a bit carried away with the novelty of it all. CBT isn't a cure for the universe. It's more latter-day Scorsese than a Kubrick masterpiece; less Agüero in injury time than Everton or Leicester on a good run. But it's brought me glimpses of a life that I didn't know existed. Like windows to an unlikely world. And even Leicester have won the Premier League once, remember.

When the sessions with my therapist came to an end, I knew things would be difficult. I was given a booklet to help me work through my fears – a series of columned sheets where I could document the duration and intensity of each OCD episode, with the aim of gradually re-working my relationship with intrusive thoughts. As with any theory put into practice, things haven't been that simple. There are days when O just won't leave me alone; it clings to the edges of every doubt that I have, and no matter how hard I try to push it into the background, it holds on for dear life, swinging and screaming like a toddler having a tantrum. And the blunt truth is, I'm not convinced I'll ever get it to leave completely. I'm not convinced we can even be totally separated.

Don't get me wrong – fuck Freud. And fuck Oedipus. Myth is the lazy man's guide to the cosmos, and the idea that mental illness can be absorbed by some ancient narrative is one of the most dangerous myths there is. But there's a space for self-reflection that isn't mired by *The Odyssey*, or the ramblings of an old, misogynistic Austrian coked-up to his eyeballs. It's called making peace with your illness. It starts with an ongoing dialogue. The final aim is not to argue with it or to cure it, but to simply acknowledge its presence – however reluctantly – whilst also acknowledging its unrivalled propensity to lie through its teeth.

It may not work for you, but at the moment, it's working for me. Along with the CBT (which I continue to practice every day) I write these letters as if I intend to send them to an old acquaintance. They are made up of words, not flesh, but they are no less a part of me than my allergy to cats, or the scar on my upper lip that's been with me since the day I learned to walk. It's not what I write that matters. It's who I am writing to. I know that O is a part of me now. It's been hanging around for too long to just disappear on command.

But I also know happiness is sometimes found in the most unexpected of places, and that having the bravery to go to such places is the secret to living the life I've been searching for since childhood.

This essay was never about saying goodbye to suffering, O. It was about learning to mine the underside of that suffering – about discovering the joys and possibilities hidden beneath its surface. It was about us. It was about *me*.

No hard feelings,

Josh

Finding Voice

Taylor Edmonds

In my early teens, I learned two pivotal things about myself: that I was mixed-race, and that I liked girls. These facts had always been there, looming in the background somewhere, but I hadn't needed to pay attention to them yet. When I started writing poetry, I realised the importance of understanding the intersections of my identity, and how those intersections impact the way I see the world and ultimately inform my writing.

I knew that some of my family were black, and some were white. I had big, curly hair like my mum and my grandad's wide nose. I also had light-olive skin and green eyes. I didn't look too different from my friends. My mum had told me about my Bajan heritage, and I didn't have any questions about what that meant.

In my favourite films and books, I was always drawn to the female characters. My friends were getting boyfriends and thinking of having sex, and my only relationship had lasted a few days, with a boy who was too afraid to hold my hand. I had crushes on boys and drunken kisses, but nothing felt like the heart-pounding firework explosions cheesy films and teen novels had taught me to expect. I wanted love that people wrote poems about.

I went to an all-girls secondary school, and there were a couple of older girls in gay relationships. They held hands in the corridors, kissed on the stairways and I was fascinated by them. I watched them intently, secretly. I heard comments from others about how 'disgusting' they were.

Once, I found a lesbian sex story on the internet, and read it over and over again, and showed it to a friend who stopped reading after a few lines and said that it made her feel sick. I nodded my head hard in agreement, and added a 'gross, innit' for good measure. I felt ashamed.

Growing up as a female, discussing my sexuality and pleasure wasn't something that was encouraged. The teaching of sex education in school was essentially an embarrassed teacher skimming over pregnancy, or awkwardly demonstrating how to put a condom on a banana, adding labels to vulva and vagina diagrams and mentioning scary STDs. I remember there being an intense pressure to lose your virginity at a young age. When entering year 9, at age 13 or 14, a friend told me that 'this was the year everyone lost it'. Most of what I had learnt about sex came from my peers, which consisted of many ill-informed rumours, and nobody expressed the same wandering mind towards other girls. To navigate these parts of myself was difficult enough without having another layer of bi-curiosity thrown into the mix. So, I tried to push these feeling to one side, hoping they wouldn't surface again, and focused on being 'normal' like everyone else around me appeared to be.

In school one day, we had to fill out a survey. Under the 'Nationality' section I hovered between the 'White British' box and the 'Mixed – White British and Black Caribbean' box. I felt conflicted. Sure, I was mixed – but mixed enough? I was mostly white, but not completely. People around me began to stand up and hand in their completed questionnaires, leaving for break time. Panicked, I ticked 'White British', scribbled it out, and ticked 'Mixed – White British and Black Caribbean'.

Since then, I have come to realise that this was a pivotal moment that I share with many other mixed-race people, especially those that are third generation descendants like myself. This box-checking dilemma was when I realised that I didn't know where I fitted in. There were a few people of colour at my school, but most of my friends were white. I didn't feel I could identify myself as the same of any of them. My friends joked that I was 'the whitest black girl they ever met'. It was harmless, but it highlighted my differences from both black and white people; I was certainly neither of them. This joke is also evidence of the extent to which people were unable to understand the concept of race beyond 'black' and 'white'. It's a lot more complex than that. In today's more multicultural society, understanding of the complexities of race is improving, though there is still progress to be made.

Being mixed-race or biracial is defined as 'the fact or state of being born to parents of different races.'[26] This is traditionally viewed as being of dual heritage, i.e. having one white parent and one black parent. But what happens to the children, like me, of these mixed-race parents? The mixed-race population is the fastest growing demographic in the UK; between 2001 and 2011 the number of people that identified as of mixed or multiple ethnicities in the UK grew from 660,000 (1%) to 1.2 million (2%).[27] With mixed-race relationships becoming more common, this increase is set to rise rapidly. This is something that has come into mainstream discussion with

---

[26] Collins English Dictionary (online).

[27] 2011 Census, Key Statistics for Local Authorities in England and Wales, released Dec 2012 (Office for National Statistics). Accessed via nationalarchives.gov.uk.

the royal marriage of Prince Harry and Meghan Markle, and more recently, the birth of their son Archie. In the run-up to Archie's birth, there was great anticipation of what a mixed-race royal baby might look like, especially as there has never been one before. A quick google search and you'll find many computer-generated images estimating what the royal baby's features will be like as he grows up – eye colour, nose shape, lips, skin tone, hair texture.

Soon after the birth of Archie, BBC Radio 5 DJ Danny Baker was fired after Tweeting a black and white picture of a well-dressed man and woman with a chimpanzee in a suit, along with the caption 'Royal baby leaves hospital.'[28] The historic racist connotation of comparing black people to apes shows a clear racist intention behind the comparison of this image with multiracial baby Archie. The fact that Archie's blackness was the main cause for concern a mere day or two after he was born, is testament to how non-whiteness is the 'other' in British society. For me, it was a stark reminder that my blackness could be seen as of equal significance. The way Meghan herself has been tirelessly hounded by the British press for everything she does is no coincidence; there are clear racial undertones to the way the media villainises her. *The Daily Mail* described her as '(almost) straight outta Compton'[29] when her relationship with Harry became news, and she continues to be branded as tainting on the royal family.

Now, at 24, I would never hover over the 'White British' box. Though I have to admit that sometimes, still, I question if I even have the 'right' to identify as mixed-race. Since writing and performing poetry, I've started to interrogate the

---

[28] 'Danny Baker fired by BBC over 'offensive' royal baby ape tweet', *The Guardian* (9th May 2019).

[29] 'EXCLUSIVE: Harry's girl is (almost) straight outta Compton', *The Daily Mail* (2nd November 2016).

term mixed-race and my own relation to it in ways I haven't before. I understand that my white friends don't feel the same sting that I do when I hear a story about racism or prejudice; for them it's not personal. I also understand that I benefit from white privilege, that certain things in life aren't as difficult for me as they are for some people in my family and other people of colour, because I'm light-skinned and white-passing.

It has taken a lot for me and for others around me to come to terms with my sexuality. I've been in long-term relationships with both women and men, and navigating these relationships in wider society are very different experiences. With my boyfriend now, I don't have to concern myself with how people will react when we hold hands in public. I don't worry about unwanted misogynistic comments from men, deal with the anxiety of telling new people who my partner is, or worse, be attacked, murdered or put in prison for being who I am, as is the case for many LGBTQ+ people all over the world.

Recently, two young women, who had been out on a date, were attacked on a bus in London after being asked to kiss by a group of boys. When they refused, the boys taunted them with various misogynistic, homophobic remarks, before physically attacking them. A photo of the women with bloody faces and clothes, went viral online.[30]

For some, this seemed a shocking thing to happen in liberal London, and until this incident, violent homophobic attacks had seemed like something faraway, that happened a long time ago in the UK or in other parts of the world. For others, this attack was not so surprising. Many women that have been in same-sex relationships came out in solidarity

---

[30] 'Gay couple beaten up on bus for refusing to kiss say they were treated as "sexual objects"', *Metro* (15th June 2019).

and talked about their experiences of misogynistic harassment on Twitter. It was all very familiar to me too. With past girlfriends, I've been asked to perform sexual acts in front of men for their entertainment and received aggressive, unwanted comments fetishising my relationships. Bisexuality is commonly hypersexualised. It's often assumed that I'm greedy, easy, and anyone's for the taking, which has led to some uncomfortable advancements and situations.

LGBTQ+ people of colour are subject to further marginalisation, as these two parts of their identity intersect. After the London homophobic attack, Chris, one of the victims, spoke out on the public outrage that followed, asking those condemning the attackers online 'Do you get outraged about all homophobia?'[31] She pointed out that the level of public outrage was because two white, feminine and cisgender LGBTQ+ people were attacked, while similar or worse attacks on non-white LGBTQ+ people do not usually prompt the same public response and make news headlines.

It's hard to know what to do with all this injustice; how to talk about it and figure out what can be done to fight it. But poetry has become a tool through which I can explore things that are difficult to articulate. When my mum tells me about her experiences with racism, I can turn them into a poem and read it to a room of people. I can write poems about love between two women that show same-sex relationships as complex and intimate as they really are, in contrast to stereotypical representations of them in TV and film. I find empowerment in this. Writing has always been something I've done; before I really knew what contemporary poetry

---

[31] Hannigan, Christine, 'You saw me covered in blood on a bus. But do you get outraged about all homophobia?', *The Guardian* (14th June 2019).

was like, I was putting words together without calling it poetry. Writing has always been a way for me to communicate my own experiences and feelings, as well as those around me. As I've gone on to be privileged enough to study creative writing at university, I've been exposed to the writing of others and connected with people that use writing in similar ways. I've become fascinated with the relationship between myself as a writer and my audience/reader, and how my poetry can be used as a means of communication. When my work sparks a response in people, when they feel they can relate to it, this forms a strange sort of intimate connection between us that runs deeper than anything I could give them in an everyday social situation.

I read the following poem, 'Exotic', at the first Where I'm Coming From open mic, a Cardiff open mic which aims to promote the work of BAME writers in Wales:

Exotic

My mother, or *brown girl*
in the school playground,
un-belonging, dirty,
don't touch.

Her first boyfriend
told her that her lips
are like small colonies,
that she tastes
like emptiness
and foreign places.

Her first boss
told her that she was exotic.

Caramel-smooth goddess
with flat-ironed, frizzy hair.

My mother felt trapped
in the casing of her own skin.
She took her nails to her forearm,
wrist to elbow crease.
Deep scratches at night,
hoping to colour herself white.

My mum grew up as one of few mixed-race people in our hometown. She has told me stories of racial abuse from her classmates at school dances, at work, and these are still things she experiences today. A story that stuck out to me the most was about her and her white friends, as primary school children, scratching her with their nails to try and change my mum's skin colour to white. It seemed such a poignant example of how deep-rooted racism is in our culture, and that these children probably thought they were helping my mum.

I didn't know what to do with these stories other than to write about them. My mum isn't a writer and I felt like they deserved to be heard. Whenever I have read this poem at a performance or open mic, people of colour have mentioned how they could to relate to my mum's experiences. This validates my purpose as a writer. There is great power in poetry when it gets people thinking, talking, connecting. These are the reasons I fell in love with writing poetry and spoken word; particularly the ways in which poetry can be used to tell stories, to speak of collective experiences and transform them into art. The poems that really strike me when reading are poems that get people talking, the ones that evoke responses and create unrest.

Through poetry I've discovered my voice, and in turn

become comfortable in the various intersections of my identity. It has become much easier to accept myself for who I am since realising that my identity is *mine*. I bring my own unique perspective to my poetry and I've grown confident in knowing that it is important that my voice is heard.

Safe Histories

Dylan Huw

The mid-1990s are everywhere, haunting me.

I'm twenty, sad and hungover, stood outside a university bookshop window where a book cover has trapped me in its sights: *1996 and the End of History*.[32] I was born in May of that year, on a cold and bright Sunday on the Ceredigion coast. That day, I was on the TV news, a stock-footage baby, archival material before I ever experienced fresh air.

Then I'm twenty-one, at Chapter Arts Centre, seeing a new body of work by the Cardiff-raised artist James Richards, having my whole mind and body blown; reacting as if electrically to the exhibition's stream of historical materials. Its images, of queer deformities, perversions and corruptions, are unattributed. Some are shot or collected by Richards, some by his collaborator Steve Reinke, but mostly they are bastard images, scattered documents of the unofficial histories which the 20th century abandoned. Cut among them are Polaroids of a younger James Richards himself, drinking beers with friends at a 1990s Cardiff Pride.

These and other queer ghosts of that era, the era of my

---

[32] David Stubbs, *1996 And The End of History* (Duncan Baird Publishers, 2016).

birth, keep replaying on my mind's screen. Days spent in a YouTube rabbit hole watching the late artist Reza Abdoh's stark, still-shocking performance pieces. Becoming hooked on Gil Cuadros' *City of God*, a memoir of the Chicano author's last young years as disease ravages Los Angeles. Some of Derek Jarman's deathbed paintings, which I see on a London gallery wall, and which make me cry.

Those artists, each so bound up with the recent history of resiliently queer artistic production, died of AIDS in 1995, 1996 and 1994, respectively.

1996's 'Fastlove', George Michael's final UK number one single, was the number one song in the UK the week I was born. (As we know, he died on Christmas Day 20 years later.) The video is set in a CGI future recognisable from any number of futurist mid-1990s cultural artefacts, with Michael as a gleeful voyeur. In today's light, his queerness appears unapologetic, carnal; a riposte against the heteronormative ideals to which male sex symbols, then as now, were expected to adhere. George wants to fuck in his BMW, to *practice the same religion* with any number of partners, winkingly withholding explicit details.

At the intersection of the era of the Gay Plague and its slow creep into the early twenty-first century's epoch of 'gay rights', here is a global superstar making no apology – no prophecy and no grand statement – arguing for pure pleasure while the world around him burns.

The era of my birth was the era of the Gay Plague's last days and thus of the great gay paradigm shift; a century into another; a closet into the liberal Western mainstream. I try to understand why I feel that era as if in my blood, on my flesh, following me everywhere I go. As inextricable from my relationship to my gayness, my privileged and 'accepted' gayness, itself.

The sense that I get to be free, as others didn't, and as many still don't, stalks me.

I want to come to terms with the bleak histories of where my freedom came from. To understand my own multi-layered privilege in relation to the struggle and ruination which might have defined a person like me only recently. I know that I am heir to the warzone of recent queer history without feeling any of its ravages materially, but receiving all the benefits of what came after: the liberal-mainstream 'acceptance' of certain kinds of queer bodies – the healthy, wealthy, usually white.

We are all heirs of something.

Gay men stopped dying, a little, in 1996. Antiretroviral combination therapy went mainstream in the U.K; the number of AIDS deaths declined for the first time since the beginning of the Plague and AIDS was no longer the leading cause of death of Americans aged 25-44. 1995, the year I was conceived, was the deadliest year on record.

I have always felt an affinity for the beginnings and endings of things. I like thinking about symbols, anniversaries, strange and accidental temporal associations.

Is it too cliché to say that gay men, generally, love nothing more than self-mythologising? Though this tendency can be damaging or short-sighted, I'm often struck by a feeling that there is no way to make sense of my own gayness – the relationship between what or who I desire and *who I am* – beyond making sense of my relationship to that lineage of queer history, my inheritance. No way outside of that question, *how we got 'here'*, those thorny and contested histories, indeed the thorny and contested 'here'.

And there is no mythology that looms larger in queer consciousness than the Stonewall Riots of June 1969. Here I am, again, it's June 2019 and this great origin story of modern gay rights and all its surrounding discourses is everywhere. It's 50 years since those riots took place, spurring the long narrative of how we now perceive 'gay rights' or 'gay politics' in the West into action.

Over time, the radicalism of the events, so long dimmed by the apoliticised rights discourses which always threaten queer liberation, has asserted itself into historical narrative. The people who fought for their existence on those Greenwich Village summer nights were not the usual grand subjects of history. Most were poor, many were trans or gender-non-conforming, some were sex workers, and a majority were non-white. They had had enough – of the police raids, of the violence, of the Mafia who ran their beloved establishment, of the microaggressions – and the rest, as they say, is history. The gay liberation movement, loosely defined as it was, followed in those riots' wake – further protests, the formation of activist groups around the world, a profoundly and rapidly increased visibility and awareness surrounding the queer person as a distinct political subject.

Inheritances define who we are, our sense of who we are in relation to the world. Thus the more clearly defined the narrative, the more we love to pay remembrance. We seek sanctuary in safe history. Even, or especially, as these safe histories elide those which are less-official, less-accepted, less-settled.

Anniversaries are all myths, in their own way.

It was in 1994 that Tony Kushner, one of America's highest-pedigree gay voices, fresh off the success of his epic two-part play, *Angels in America*, published his essay 'A Socialism of the Skin (Liberation, Honey!)' in *The Nation*. Its appearance, in that prestigious magazine's July 4th issue, defined the battle lines he saw forming in gay cultural politics at the time.

In the essay, Kushner outlines a fork in the road, referencing some of the leading mainstream-conservative gay thinkers and commentators of his time. On the one hand, gay liberation, in the tradition of the most prominent AIDS-era activists, meaning the liberation of all queer people from the ravages of capitalism, with a particular emphasis on doubly or triply subjugated people, i.e. those without access to other types of privilege. On the other, was what Kushner saw as the conservatism of the emerging gay rights battles, which play out exclusively among privileged corridors of power and have legal and judicial battles as their sole focus – the right to marry, to 'serve' your country, to bear children like straight people do. To be normal, like straight people are. In other words, to live respectably.

As I write this, it is 25 years almost to the day since the publication of Kushner's essay; we are exactly as far removed from his premoninitive analyses as was he from the events of June 1969 at the Stonewall Inn.

I wonder what it is about this that makes me feel so claustrophobic.

Where we are now is a complicated issue. Pride month in 2019 has been the biggest yet – more visible, more mainstreamed and more hotly debated than any before it. The South Wales Police had their cars in rainbow flags; the UK Home Office carried a month-long Pride-coloured social media campaign. Seemingly every bank and corporation acknowledged the celebrations; what we were all celebrating, however, no one could tell you exactly.

I am not interested in making any argument about how preposterous it is for such symbols of state and corporate power to denote so flimsily that they 'accept' people like me.

I am not interested in an 'acceptance' that looks like a rainbow-covered police car or a Goldman Sachs float at Pride. 'People like me' constitute a much narrower sliver of the queer populace than is usually acknowledged. As a middle-class, white, able-bodied, Russell-Group-educated, twinkly conventional-looking, late-1990s-born cis-gendered man from Aberystwyth, my gayness has never remotely been a question of 'acceptance'. The innate privilege with which I have been lucky to live my 20-something life so far means that the entire grammar of 'acceptance' and 'oppression' cannot resonate on any material basis. I don't have a 'coming out' story. I was never bullied, not really. HIV-AIDS was treatable as soon as I was born. I see the faces of white, middle-class gay men in media and prestigious public life all the time.

My gayness – my 2019 gayness – is boring, uninteresting, predictable, even. As a political subject in 2019, I am no more minoritised than a straight person who otherwise shares my demographic profile.

In the first part of 'A Socialism of the Skin,' Kushner's kick, which probably reads more profoundly on the piece's 25th anniversary than it has at any other point since its publication, describes a desolate near future world in which gay marriage and serving in the military – that is, the right for certain gay people to be folded into the ancient structural logic of a capitalist, heteropatriarchal world – are the extent of the gay rights movement's wins.

Our world – at least as miserably and thoroughly ravaged as 1994 could have ever imagined – may have room for a liberal consensus of 'acceptance' of queer people, but Kushner's overall premonitions, it seems to me, is how the last twenty-five years of gay politics has transpired.

I am now 'normal'. Many queer people are not. And still

this haunting. The ghosts of recent queer history's activism, art and politics follow me everywhere.

What could it mean to embody this history within myself? To carry it with me as I encounter this changing world? My gayness may be as banal as any other part of my character or identity, but I am still a part of this inescapable lineage.

In James Richards' work, which speaks to me so profoundly, these inheritances are explored as archival detritus. He works with appropriated materials, constructing crudely edited, oblique and frequently mystifying audiovisual works which render it impossible to distinguish between form and content, inviting confusion and restless inspiration in equal measure. In *What weakens the flesh is the flesh itself*, commissioned as part of Richards' exhibition representing Wales at the 2017 Venice Biennale and made in collaboration with Reinke, you are left with an assemblage of fragments that build an imagistic portrait of queer histories and their legacies. It explores, above all, how these histories are passed from generation to generation as images. As its starting point the work uses photographs from the archives of Albrecht Becker, a gay man persecuted in Nazi Germany who obsessively took self-portraits of the various forms of body modification undertaken by him and those in his circle.

This choppily edited montage gradually patchworks a sense of history being communicated not as an ontological straight line but as necessarily fluid, as mutable; as queer. A world in which queerness is a matter of 'acceptance' is a world far outside of the one created by Richards' and Reinke's film.

After months spent grappling with that work, and moving to Cardiff in 2018, I became obsessed by *Race d'Ep*, a semi-forgotten documentary mini-series from 1979. It speaks to the same desire, to see queer inheritances as ones which might

71

be unruly, perverse, dirty – unofficial – as much as neutered or assimilated. Created by writer Guy Hocquenghem, who is often regarded as a father of French queer theory, in collaboration with the radical video artist Lionel Soukaz, it traces a history of gay desire as it had been imaged in the preceding century or two. It is dizzying.

I want to be confounded by the legacy which I am a part of. I want to feel it in my body, not to see its symbols awkwardly co-opted by Pride floats or simplified narratives. I want to discover new ways of feeling my own bodily relation to my gayness (a gayness of privilege and mainstreamed, pragmatic political battles) in relationship to the world which I have inherited.

Five days before I was born, South Africa became the first country in the world to explicitly prohibit discrimination based on sexual orientation in its national constitution. Since then, most western countries have taken similarly official steps to formally 'accept' gay people.

There is no way of discussing gayness in 2019 that isn't in some way coloured by the tension between our recent brutal past and the Western liberal consensus which allows gay men such as myself to live in something like 'freedom'. If myth and metaphor are the defining registers of talking about gayness, this awkward tension might be the defining register of *being* privileged and gay today.

Of course, I am grateful for the normativist rights battles that have been won. It's easy to forget that there is no greater privilege than being (coding as) *normal*. Equality is not liberation, and certainly not for everyone, but it remains *an* important strategy.

The End of History, as quaintly promised by the 1990s, never happened, and our planet kept changing at an accelerating pace as new wars and crises and paranoias asserted themselves. The empty, capitalistic symbolism to which queer history often feels reduced to seems oblivious to this.

Growing up I was obsessed with the New Queer Cinema movement, a loosely defined congregation of non-hetero North American film-makers. Artists like Gregg Araki, who spent the early nineties making angry, disease-inflected masterpieces of teen disillusionment like *Totally Fucked Up* and *Nowhere*. Beyond simply representing gay and queer characters at their centre, these films explored the boundaries of transgression, existing self-consciously as part of a widely-felt sense of nihilism and disillusionment within queer subcultures at the time. (And The End of History was never so horny.)

Arguably the movement was already past-it by the time I was born; it existed as part of an anti-normative fury or not at all.

What comes after the end of the End of History? We might as well ask: how can a planet burn and drown at the same time?

I'm exhausted. And still this claustrophobia. Still these ghosts haunt me.

Maybe it is because we are all asking the wrong questions.

I couldn't shake the book I'd seen in the window, *1996 and the End of History*. One day, after I received my final student loan instalment, I decided to go into the shop and buy it. I thought maybe reading it would slay the ghost. But, by then, the copies had all sold out.

Colonial Thinking, Education, Politics, Language and Race... From the Personal to the Political

Isabel Adonis

My father was from Guyana in the Caribbean. He was a black man whose attitudes, manners, language and culture were all those of a colonial Victorian English gentleman. My mother and her side of the family, with whom I mainly grew up, were Welsh speaking from Bethesda, North Wales. She spoke English to her husband and to her children, but to her Welsh relatives and neighbours, a mix of Welsh and English, where she was more comfortable. Her Welsh persona was livelier and emotionally expressive. It was like there were two people inside of each of them.

My father's conflict was between his upbringing as a British, middle-class, cultural administrator and authority of the Empire, and the truth, discovered in his rejection as such in Britain, of his black, Guyanese identity. My mother's was between the Welsh culture that she felt had rejected her and the English culture that she both desired and despised. She had been raised in an orphanage in Caernarfon and had lost her place in her own community. This ambivalence towards Englishness was where they met and where the family lived, and constitutes the essence of the colonised mind and colonised culture that only rejection makes conscious.

In school in Llandudno, both primary and secondary, my teachers were a mixture of Welsh and English, but the medium was generally English with the same smattering of Welsh as I had been used to hearing at home. So for me, as a child, I communicated mainly in English, but Welsh was always there in the background as part of my culture and communication; at home, at school and in the neighbourhood. This was the Welsh I understood and which provided a certain security for me. I learnt prayers, songs and much more. I could only speak a little Welsh but I could understand a good deal. For me there was no 'English' or 'Welsh', just this mix of language without real borders.

By the time I got to Bangor University at the end of the seventies to do a degree course in Education things were very different. By then the whole tone of the language had changed; it actually sounded very different to me. My Welsh relatives had always been very accepting and accommodating but I found increasingly that linguistic frontier lines between Welsh and English were being drawn. The medium of education was still English, but I couldn't help but notice how the student community was split into English and Welsh speakers, and that this reflected the division of the schools where we would do our teachers practice and presumably pursue our careers into English medium or Welsh medium. Despite my 'Welsh' upbringing I was no longer Welsh enough. I was now an 'other', lumped in with the English. The 'we' no longer meant me. I retreated to Bethesda – my mother's birthplace.

What was happening in Wales was a struggle for national freedom. I recalled the words of Franz Fanon in his seminal speeches collected as *The Wretched of the Earth*:

> After a century of colonial domination we find a culture which is rigid in the extreme, or rather what we find are the dregs of culture, its mineral strata… the negation of the native's culture, the contempt for any manifestation of culture whether active or emotional and the placing outside the pale of all specialised branches of organisation contribute to breed aggressive patterns of conduct in the native.[33]

Bethesda was such an interesting place to live. It related directly to what Fanon was expressing. There were the old cultural forms, the chapel, the shops, the Penrhyn Strike, my mum's relations – the old culture as passed on to me by my mother. Sitting side by side with the old ways of doing things was the emergence of new forms of artistic expression. The English hippies, who had been renegades of colonial culture and refugees from England, had brought with them new cultural possibilities with their music and art and there had been a merging of cultures with the local Welsh youth. For instance in 1977 there was the Ogwen Valley Fair where English and Welsh bands were on the bill. There were also gigs at Plas Coch in Anglesey and the Glanrafon pub in Bangor. Les Morrison (1956-2011) was at the centre of it, producing Welsh and English music at his studio in Bethesda. However, there was still an antagonism, a tension, between the English incomers and the native Welsh. The call was for the English to go home. It was literally written (in English) on the wall.

I had gone there to find a home, but rather than finding support and acceptance, my family were marginalised by

---

[33] Franz Fanon, Speech at the Congress of Black African Writers (www.marxists.org), also found in *The Wretched of the Earth* (London: Pelican, 1959).

some and even humiliated and racially abused in this divided community. Fortunately it was not everyone – vestiges of the old welcoming culture remained. Rejected by Welsh and English communities I was forced into an awareness of black identity. I changed my name from Williams because I realised it was a slave name and I discovered another connection, that the Pennants, owners of Bethesda quarry, also had slaves in the Caribbean. These things rather complicate any notion of innocence connected to the idea that Wales is a colony.

The duality of Welsh identity as both coloniser and colonised naturally leads to the merging of cultures already described, but as Fanon observes, the cultural elite resists: 'The colonialist specialists do not recognise these new forms and rush to the help of the traditions of the indigenous society. It is the colonialists who become the defenders of the native style.'[34]

In Bethesda and elsewhere, these specialists – mainly intellectuals – were quick to adopt the Welsh language as the main expression of the culture. These 'defenders of the native style' sought to preserve the real thing. They gathered the jewels of the old Welsh culture and set out to protect them at whatever cost. The Welsh language was promoted everywhere and especially in schools. In terms of the cost, we have a stymying of living culture, which was never pure and not static. The cost of preserving a pure Welsh language is that it becomes marginalised and not the Welsh that ordinary people speak. They in their turn became the new colonialists while imagining themselves to be defending the native culture. My father did the same thing in his native Guyana. He studied sacred art in Africa and in Guyana he concentrated his attention to the study of ancient petroglyphs.

---

[34] Ibid.

A living culture is a very messy business, which is always changing and contradicting itself. It is not static – any more than a living language is. Paradoxically, the instinct to preserve the bones of the tradition and the purity of the mother tongue comes out of the colonial mindset and is opposed to the creative innovation of the very people who embody that tradition. In this case the native Welsh.

Just as the colonial outgrowth that is the BBC sought for many years – and arguably still covertly does – to impose upon the varied linguistic traditions of English the rigid discipline of 'the Queen's English' and 'received pronunciation', so it is the colonial instincts of the Welsh intellectual that seek to repress the natural flow between the Welsh and English languages. Their aim is to preserve a 'pure' tradition that was only ever the result of an imaginary total isolation.

So this is the danger; the nation identifies itself in contrast with the colonial oppressor and the very struggle for an independent entity for Wales leads back to the recreation of that oppression internally. Instead of liberating itself, Wales oppresses itself and calls that independence. A superficial but telling example of this evolution is the desire to express authentic identity through mimicry, as in the case of the full English breakfast which is now known as a full Welsh breakfast (which is the same, apart from in some cases the addition of laverbread).

Likewise, the devolved government of Wales has located itself in the southern, urban, industrial port of Cardiff to supposedly represent the largely rural country of Wales, recreating all the unrepresentative biases of London in Welsh form. From whence an unrepresentative image of Welsh-ness, a constrictive and divisive image, is being imposed by policies that seek to maintain the purity of the culture by conditional grants to the arts, and especially through the transformation of the education system.

Following in Fanon's footsteps, Paulo Freire in the *Pedagogy of the Oppressed,* says: 'Men and women rarely admit their fear of freedom openly, however, tending to camouflage it … by presenting themselves as the defenders of freedom … But they confuse freedom with the maintenance of the status quo…'[35] Like Fanon, he calls for the oppressed to explore a national critical consciousness rather than nationalism in order that they might liberate themselves and their oppressor as well because, '[o]nly power that springs from the weakness of the oppressed will be sufficiently strong to free both.'[36]

The educating of a nation is not a neutral act, and in the case of Wales its attempt to recolonise its own language and culture has led to a policy to increase the number of Welsh speakers. By 2050 it plans to increase Welsh-medium education by a third, raising the level to 30% taught exclusively in Welsh.

Colin Baker, a former Professor of Education at Bangor University, has argued for the separation of those children who speak English as a first language from those whose first language is a minority language. He correctly points to the fact that each group has different needs: English is a global language of power and influence whereas the possibility of retaining Welsh for instance as a minority language remains a limited one. He foresees that in the long term that Welsh children might lose their minority language.[37]

This, however, is the colonialist specialist that Fanon points to, seeking to preserve the native culture from the

---

[35] Paulo Freire, *Pedagogy of the Oppressed* (London: Penguin, 1996).

[36] Ibid.

[37] Colin Baker, in his 'Foreword' for *Language in Multilingual Wales* (Bangor University: College of Education and Lifelong Learning, 2009).

depredations of his own culture's domination; a voice that comes from the educated colonised as much as from the coloniser. Because to be educated *means* to be en-cultured in the colonising culture, not the colonised. Baker proudly informs us that Wales is a world leader in language planning and in bilingual education as if it is a *good* thing and a *doable* thing to plan the voice of a people.

In the context of neocolonialism where language acquisition is once more being controlled by the state, a policy of separation has inevitably created nationalist tendencies and, when combined with a dearth of ethnic minority teachers in Welsh schools, offers ground for misunderstanding and even casual racism.

My own teacher's practice was traumatic. No assistance was given to me and I spent any spare time hiding in the toilet until eventually I was forced out of the school; an outsider blamed for circumstances beyond my control.

I feel children are indirectly being taught how to be nationalist, to identify with being Welsh, thus creating *others*. The trend towards schools which will be exclusively Welsh exacerbates racial division; the English and the ethnic minorities. In a recent BBC television programme about the effects of devolution entitled 'The Story of Wales', no mention was made of ethnic minorities, the disabled, gypsies or the LGBT community. Wales was represented as exclusively white.

In practice, the division is between Welsh speakers and all others. 'Others', including my own Wales-born and Welsh descended children, are not welcomed into Welsh-language schools. A head teacher suggested once that my daughters would be better off in a 'multicultural' school in Bangor. The practice betrays the concern for a separation to maintain purity, and not to establish any kind of equality or liberation.

What the Welsh are doing to their nationalism is recreating a British nationalism with the same attitude – leading the world – which is divisive and exclusive: the very same quality they despise in the English. Cultural commentators are right in that the English language is not in danger of dying out and the Welsh language is. They propose a separation of languages and a separation of people who speak them. However, this is a departure from the reality where people mix the languages. Neither culture nor language (nor skin colour for that matter) are separate: there is no demarcation or monolithic culture. How more colonial can you be? Separation implies purity and such notions in relation to culture can lead to a hostile environment of segregation and apartheid.

My father came to London and tried to be a Victorian colonialist, and then he tried to be a colonialist in Africa and finally he returned to Guyana and became the *omnipotent administrator*.[38] He would never accept his mixedness; his black skin/white mask. My mother would never accept her Englishness and nor will I. I am not mixed, I am not a minority or a foreigner or an outsider or a sub-culture. I am complete. *Yr wyf gartref*. I am *Gymraeg*.

---

[38] Eldridge Cleaver, *Soul on Ice* (London: Jonathan Cape, 1969).

A Reluctant Self

Ranjit Saimbi

I

It is strange how certain memories persist. Though the scene may be indistinct and abstract, the sense of the memory, the emotions it evokes, are inviolable and pristine. I remember my first visit to a Cardiff Gurdwara in the same way. I don't remember the details, just smudges seen at the crook of my mother's knees. Perhaps I am burying my face into the folds of her sari and digging my heels in at the cusp of the prayer hall entrance – who knows now – but it is reluctance that I feel, a deep and permeating reluctance that has barely dimmed.

The Gurdwara in Cardiff is housed in a repurposed Victorian church, constructed with squat and substantial masonry. A decline in Christian worship, and a more godly Sikh diaspora led to the Gurdwara's founding in 1977. Why not let this building be used for a more religiously virile group's worship? Strip out the pews, replace one religion's altar for another, let the figures in the stained-glass windows observe other people's customs and rituals.

During the week it looks like any suburban Cardiff street;

rows of hemmed-in terraced houses and the dour grey church edifice resting on its haunches. The only clue that something might be different is a flagpole dressed in a tangy, orange flag, emblazoned with Khanda. Each Sunday morning, worshippers descend on the suburban street, which can barely cope with the influx of parked cars. Women are in bright salwar kameez and sarees, the men wear paghs and have wiry beards. The girls wear chunnis, and the boys have ramalah on their heads. They appear in the neighbourhood and meander toward the converted church – a brightly-clothed and brown-skinned mirage in the unenthusiastically grey street.

I think most of that reluctance came from the disjunction between my lived life, and what felt to me like a jarring and alien intrusion, as jarring as those exotic worshippers in a suburban street. I didn't get this Sikh stuff. I didn't get why, on Sundays, I had to wrap some cloth around my head and sit in a prayer hall with all these people I didn't know, reciting prayers. We grew up in Thornhill and I went to the local primary school. I did all the usual things. I got a bike with stabilisers that clattered around the street in the summer sun. I painted rocks. I kicked balls over neighbour's fences. I knocked on friends' doors to see if they would come out to play. I grew out of stabilisers and careered around the neighbourhood with my pack of street friends. We made fires with deodorant cans, we hid our secret files in secret dens, and aimed water pistols at the open windows of passing cars.

You see, the Gurdwara is a place of unspoken rules and ritual. When you enter the prayer hall you notice these rules that govern worship, although they are never explained. Men and women sit separately, cross-legged on white sheets. All heads are covered, men are turbanned; women are draped in chunnis. At the front of the hall is something like an altar, a gazebo structure which stands above a raised platform, whereon a holy man sits singing from the holy book. He waves a horsehair brush which purifies the air around him. Conscientious worshippers rock back and fore to the holy man's chants in a strange, almost stupefied trance, sometimes echoing his chants in more muffled, less distinct tones. It was apparent to me, even then, that these people were bound by an understanding of ancient customs that I did not have access to.

As a child, looking in on this theatre of worship I felt perturbed. When one enters the prayer hall you must walk along a carpeted aisle between the male and female worshippers. It is a public act of worship. For the actors who had learnt their lines, they would walk with slow dignity and intention, and when they reached the altar, prostrate themselves on the ground in front of the holy book, rears in the air, with the prayer hall watching. Before stepping out into that prayer hall, I felt that same trepidation, as though about to plunge into an icy sea, or like an actor, before launching themselves on stage before an expectant audience, except that I had never learned my lines.

II

Although I had never felt a visceral or intuitive sense of belonging toward that place of worship, I could, in a pragmatic sort of way see the purpose of these regulated relations. In particular, I could see why my father's generation clung hard and fast to their culture.

My father grew up in Uganda, and was part of the diaspora that was expelled by Amin in the 1970s. In those days, especially in Uganda, communal bonds superseded almost every walk of life. Old friendships from ancestral villages in India were transposed onto the idyllic Kampalan countryside. Houses would be packed with family and friends. Kids would roam around eating ripe, swollen mangoes off trees. They would catch snakes and hew spears. On weekends, disparately connected communities of people would pile into flatbed trucks and 4x4s and head into the jungle for barbeques. There were local clubs, and annual competitions. Business relations were forged communally and were forthcoming. By all accounts it was Edenic. I recall watching an old BBC interview with a Ugandan Asian shopkeeper. The interviewer asked his questions in the distinctive received pronunciation of the day, but the respondent's answers were misty eyed, as though hypnotised by the beauty of the Ugandan life he was describing. It was a perfect time. A red hot sun, a thriving mercantile community, which had crossed the Indian Ocean and prospered. They were the adventurers who had discovered their Eldorado.

When Amin made his decree, it would have been these familial bonds of kinship that cushioned the blow. When all of those families disembarked from planes on British runways, they would have been struck by the cold. So different from those Kampalan summers, and clubhouse games (like holidaying colonials). But at least they had each other. At least your dad's uncle has a house in London you can stay at, or you have a second cousin that you could go travelling with, or even a gang from Kampala for when you head to university: thingy's daughter or your friend's son. It was a far less atomised way of behaving and relating; you could trust people because you knew their history. It made sense that dad wanted us to go to Gurdwara when he grew up like this.

The expectation for people of that generation, was that these sprawling informal bonds that tied communities together would continue to function in much the same way, and to a large extent, for many they still do. A sense of community is borne out of these shared personal histories. Communities, after all, are formed from shared experience. For my parents' generation, community provided a sense of safety and security, and even more so, cultural continuity in a different country and amidst much turbulence. The shared lives with others, the shared milestones and touchpoints, the shared language and dress, all provided a mutually reinforcing conception of self, which could navigate and survive its newly-acquired migrant status.

III

In order to move through this Sikh world, you needed to be socialised and oriented within it in the correct way. My reluctance to enter the prayer hall was just one red-flag to any policer of this on-boarding process. I was a frequent breaker of the unspoken rules, but never because I intended to. There is nothing more unjust than the unintentional sin, and the reprimand that comes with it. There you are minding your own business, when unbeknownst to you, your merely existing in a certain way is deeply offending the senses of a policer. They might indignantly reprimand you, and then you might remember the shame and blood rushing to your cheeks for all your days on earth to come.

There are many examples from my recollection to choose from. The most frequent unthinking offence was forgetting to wear a ramal. If you've ever had a brush with Sikhism in your religious studies class, you would know that Sikhs are never meant to cut their hair, and that devotees should keep their heads covered in the Gurdwara (at all times). Well, my first error was to have my hair cut, thereby delineating me from the most pious of boys who would wear turbans. But even so, you should have your hair covered in the Gurdwara, and for a boy with short hair, that means a ramal – or, to literally everybody else, a bandana. It was the sort of thing that I would frequently forget as a child. Invariably, we would be rushing to get to Gurdwara on time, and arriving late and out of breath, as I took a seat in the prayer hall, my crime would dawn on me. As I sat there in a knot of tension, visualising the judgment of the surrounding pious folk, a stern, bearded, turbaned man would appear and give me his indignant reprimand. I was disrespectful. I was late. I did not go to Punjabi class. I mumbled my prayers.

Another unintentional sin. Partway through the service, there would be the prayer. This was the same prayer that my mum taught us before we went to school, it is the same prayer I said at night, whispering to myself before sleep. It is the same prayer I sometimes say now. When the moment came, the younger members of the congregation would gather at the front of the prayer hall and recite the prayer. Except, when I began reciting the prayer, that I knew by rote to such an extent that I could spill it out without a moment's hesitation, it felt different. The Punjabi that I did not understand anyway felt different. Consonants were different. Vowels were different. Spoken out loud, and not whispered in my head, it was different. And even worse, the prayer was recited beyond the prayer I knew. Like a cartoon character that has run off the edge of a cliff with its limbs still whirring, I mouthed and mumbled my way through, until gravity finally took hold. When the prayer ended I was relieved. I could leave the front of the prayer hall and return to sitting in anonymity until I could go home. But then the stern, bearded, turbaned man appeared to give me his indignant reprimand. This is why you should go to Punjabi class. This is why you should be on time.

How disrespectful that you do not know your own prayers. How shameful it is for you to disrespect the holy word.

I am sure that to some readers I *do* seem disrespectful. It wouldn't be that difficult to learn a prayer or to remember your ramal, just to keep the peace at least. Play the role and get on with it, no harm, no foul. Maybe. Maybe not. But why should a person be compelled to do things if they do not agree with the explanations? What if, when you explain the deep spiritual significance of something to me, I still disagree? What if to me, it feels like I am becoming a lie? I'm sure that to the stern, bearded, Sikh on-boarding officer I was the height of self-indulgence; a slave to my ego, and a slovenly Sikh. *If you don't know where you come from, then you'll never know where you're going.* That was the sort of thing he'd say. Or, *you might think that you're right about these things now, but just you wait till you're older, young man.*

IV

Now that I am older, I can look back on my relationship with my Sikh culture and heritage with a more self-aware eye. Where some might expect a resolution of sorts, some sort of melting-pot of identities where the sum is more than their constituent parts, there is in fact an outsider's critical gaze. I have silently un-coupled myself from the Sikh parts of myself, and let them drift away from me, carried off on their own current.

I have no doubt that some who take succour from their ancestral heritage would find this singular and lonely. Why reject the comfort of ancestral bonds, the historical or social co-ordinates that orient oneself? And for what? What shall fill this inevitable vacuum, they might ask? I have always found that there is a rigidity to this conception of self. The self which is too bound up with its cultural baggage is one constrained by expectation, whether explicitly or implicitly, and I have always found that world smaller and tighter around the collar. Rather, I prefer the freedom of the iterating self. The self as journey. The self as canvas. In this way, literature has provided a framework for me to make whole the varying fragments of identity. I suppose that's precisely what a poem is. A masterful poet is able to patch together seemingly disparate and disconnected words and images to make a coherent and unique whole. Experiences and anecdotes that are keenly felt at the beginning are re-contextualised by those that follow later, and all of these reframed and seen afresh by the new again, and again, and again. The self to me then, is a constantly moving point on the horizon, never still, and never beset by ossifying expectations.

This approach to constructing the self has not always been easy. At times, the differences between younger memories lived and those of my present self have been so stark that it seems the only common factor is that I have been the cypher through which they have been experienced. Often as an adult, when I am forced by familial obligation to take up these Sikh parts of myself beyond where I have placed them, the internal monologue that runs through my mind becomes cynical. Where I perceive these events to be tyrannical or not grounded in purpose, I revert back to that stubborn child at the threshold of the prayer hall.

I recall a particular ceremony between a Sikh and Hindu bride and groom. Back at the groom's house (a drive halfway across the country), tired and exhausted, we jammed into their conservatory, with the groom's family and extended family. Space had been cleared, tables and chairs pushed to the periphery and the bride and groom manhandled into a sitting position on the floor, perhaps four feet from each other.

What happens next is quite strange. An auntie (generic term for loud woman who seems to have some sort of familial status) appears with a watermelon – a big beast of a thing (watermelon not the auntie), and commands the newlyweds to roll this melon between each other. This is an icebreaker, she announces. In the olden days, when brides were very young, they would be nervous and not even know their husbands sometimes, so this would be a way for the couple to get to know each other!

And so the newlywed couple, by all accounts, typical young adults in every respect, are rolling a watermelon between each other, on a conservatory floor, somewhere in England on a damp spring day. Never mind the simple weirdness of being okay with a ceremony that takes its symbolic significance from child bride games. They are suspending rationality to please an outmoded fiction to which their tribe holds steadfast to. Of course, nearly all cultures and religions have these strange and abstracted rituals, but you won't find me rolling watermelons around the floor on my big day.

When I see these rituals, that I find jarring and absurd, I see their brittleness and vulnerability. I have a theory that often migrant cultures hold more steadfastly to these conservative practices than their native counterparts. The migrant is concerned with losing their sense of identity and so is deeply nostalgic, constantly reliving customs and rituals which they recall from childhood. Whereas a more confident native culture can absorb and morph without the same paranoia.

In truth, customs are handed down from generation to generation, tweaked here, added to there. Not hard rock like things, but bendy and porous, and therefore, not beyond the realms of critical thought. Sure, the community structure is the Bank of England that stands behind the value of this stuff and lends it authority, but these are all just habits copied in some form or another through the ages. The customs which become too rigid and outlast their purpose should be left to wither on the branch of time, not allowed to become a rod on the back of generation after generation.

I always think that cuisine is the opposite of this brittle and vulnerable sense of cultural identity. The unbroken chain of recipes passed from generations of mothers to daughters is an example of cultural batton-passing that has true purpose and grounding. I relish memories of my mother's cooking; shared meals as a family; buttery dhals, and freckled rotis. This is shared experience, it is immediate and experienced through the senses. It does not need heavy-handed explanation.

Which is to say that I see that there is value in some of these structures. At a different wedding, I saw refugees from Uganda who had not seen each other in over thirty years, drinking together and joyfully reunited. They were pulling unaired memories from the past into the present. Dusty anecdotes full of hilarity, binding the teller and listeners together to something shared that was beyond their day to day lives. In short, it was quite beautiful. But, these scenes always make me think about the shortcomings of these migrant cultures – how often do they really serve the totality of their practitioners? How often are their members allowed to be and become themselves in their entirety? This culture I speak of might be home for others, but it is not for me.

My Other(ed) Self

Özgür Uyanık

A key question for me, a Turkish-born writer raised in the United Kingdom, is whether or not BAME practitioners in the UK are truly able to express themselves freely without the danger of othering themselves in the process. The story of how I managed to make myself foreign to my own cultural heritage – how I became 'othered' – begins with an epiphany. Having read quite a few contemporary female Turkish novelists in translation, I realised with a gnawing sense of guilt that I had been avoiding novels by Turkish men, especially the well-established writers of the twentieth century. It felt vaguely as if I had an axe to grind with these men but the reason remained elusive, buried in my subconscious, until I started to dig for potential answers.

I moved to the UK with my architect parents when I was aged six. My younger sister and I were simply expected to pick up the language as we went along and we did. Before that, our infancy in Turkey was spent in an unquestioningly patriarchal society where female relatives spoke of 'growing up to be big and strong like your father' and men were routinely tasked with opening jar lids, cooking meat over hot coals and sacrificing their good cheer to deal with local aggressions against their clan, whether it be a fleeing burglar or a disrespectful tradesman. Men had an appealingly distinct place in the scheme of things and I began by identifying strongly with the prescribed masculinity – machismo and all – with a vision of my future self as 'big and strong'. However, as I grew up, I saw that the women in my family had the better story arc. These women – my mother, sister, grandmother, aunts and female cousins – all had an adversarial position in the status quo from the get go, with weightier obstacles to conquer than the men. My grandmother exemplified the notion of the female rising above the limitations set by the hierarchy. She had withstood an arranged marriage to a man fifteen years her senior and carved out a career as a teacher before entering politics. She acted and spoke of her journey as a woman of the modern Turkish Republic, risen from the ashes of a defunct empire, who had once been in the presence of our founding father Atatürk himself. On the other hand, the men in my family seemed to deal mostly in self-serving anecdotes and jokes, privileged with an identity based on their gender. Maybe then – when it came to Turkish literature – I reasoned that I ought not to bother with the thoughts and feelings of long-dead men who had sailed through life with everything seemingly tipped in their favour. In so far as social fairness was concerned, men had the upper hand in almost every sphere save for the theatre of war. Could that one inequity justify all the others? Peevishly perhaps, I felt not.

I took these thoughts and feelings with me as I stepped inside a bookstore in Bodrum in the south west of Turkey recently. It's where my mother has been living and working since her divorce almost three decades earlier. In the eighties, she had conducted her own struggle to compete in a man's world at the architectural firm she worked at in London, impeded by – of all people – her own husband. This sort of wrong made me feel less inclined to express solidarity with my own sex or sympathise with the travails of men, including my father. But when he passed away recently, a certain kinship between us developed posthumously – a hitherto unexamined connection between father and son. I started to wonder: had I been simply a petulantly angry boy who had not measured up to his father and therefore created a watchful distance from all things masculine – a pre-emptive rejection as self-defence?

I certainly felt something very deeply the day I stood in my father's freshly dug grave and his shroud-encased body was passed down to me and the municipal gravedigger, as is customary. We laid his body to rest on top of his own father's remains, separated by a few inches of soil and several decades. When the grave was filled and everyone else had drifted away, I stood staring at the place he was buried, paralysed by the thought that walking off was tantamount to abandoning him forever. In those moments of confused distress, I was unable to formulate a way to honour his memory – what was *his* narrative?

From that point on, I began to reflect on my father's struggles instead of dismissing them as an inferior category of suffering. He had grown up the youngest by 10 years in a large family; his mother had given birth to him when she was 40. The year was 1945 so this was somewhat of a shameful occurrence. He was in today's parlance 'an accident' and was raised by his older sister. His father passed away when he was nine years old and my father often reminded me that the only sign of affection he had received from him, once, was a pat on the head. Rejected by his mother and ignored by his father, it should not surprise anyone that he had difficulties showing affection to others. To my discredit, I never could find it in me to forgive him that flaw. Following his death however, having rendered him a fallible human being in my mind and deserving of empathy as much as the women in my family, I began to try and excavate my suppressed consciousness as I scanned the shelves in the bookstore. I wondered what he had tried to convey to us as children all those times he had wistfully, out of nowhere, quoted lines from Turkish poets or movingly sung a few lines from a *Türkü* (Turkish folk song). What sort of connection was he trying to make when he handed over a slim, worn paperback from his own library without explanation? It seemed that literature and song, and the Turkish culture that had animated his soul, overlooked by me into adulthood, was now a very good way for me to understand his condition and, by extension, mine.

Triggered by the bereavement, I felt compelled to reconnect with my father through the literature of my own country, and deal with the fact that it was a male-centric perspective later on. Not understanding or knowing the provenance of lines from poems and songs that my father used to quote with such feeling, and the books that he casually handed to me that I barely glanced at had become a source of embarrassment. In the bookshop, a sense of missed opportunity overwhelmed me as I stared at the hundreds of volumes of Turkish fiction and poetry that had come before me and would be there long after I was gone. I needed to get in touch with my cultural heritage. With the impenetrable barrier of death between us, I yearned to hear my father tell me his thoughts about Yaşar Kemal, Fikret Adil, İlhan Berk, Nazim Hikmet, Bedri Rahmi Eyüboğlu, Zülfü Livaneli, Can Yücel or Orhan Veli. These names conjured up an unexplored domain of thought and experience that my father had only hinted at. I felt I was on the cusp of something miraculous – that feeling of opening a portal to a quasi-foreign world, uncannily familiar, that I could legitimately call home. There was a past in those pages that had been alive and vital for millions of Turks over the preceding century yet I had become separated and then, over time, alienated from a rich background through various happenstances. How had this reluctance to explore my own tradition transpired for someone who had aspirations of being a Turco-British writer?

I submit that the disavowal of the masculine as outlined above occurred in parallel to a process of holistic self-othering that had shaped my formative years in the UK. In fact, this alignment with the feminine may have obfuscated, in retrospect, a slow and steady Anglicisation. Of course, I could hardly blame my young self for gravitating towards a western leaning mind-set when the Turkish national consciousness since its formal inception in 1923 aspired to 'modernise' as its Anatolian, or eastern, intricacies and clan-like cultural paternalism fell away (the irony that the man who had this vision in the first place was named *Father of the Turks* by a grateful populace came into sharper focus only later). This desired societal progress meant, amongst other things, equality between the sexes and a rejection of the macho Mediterranean mores that blighted the psyche of every Turkish male including, I believed then, its writers. Conceivably I was being too hard on my cultural inheritance because I was unwittingly being steered by the Anglo-Saxon perception of my own country through the British norms and education system.

During the difficult years of alienation in secondary school I was surrounded by mostly English and English-born ethnic minorities who had a deeper connection to the UK than I did. Lacking any sense of belonging in the host country, I was mapping onto my plastic brain a foreigner's idea of an image of Turkishness that I felt needed to be aligned with so that I might flourish there. After all, we were lucky to have escaped the military oppression and political chaos in Turkey during the eighties to find safe harbour in the UK. Had we therefore subconsciously performed the role of grateful immigrants (technically we were expatriates) by embracing Britishness to the detriment of our Turkishness? I felt instinctively, as I stood in the store with an armful of books in Bodrum, that I had strayed too far from an original sense of self, and that I had allowed my identity to be steered under a 'Western gaze' that insidiously infected my taste in literature. Consequently, I had to read the writings of these Turkish men in the original language to learn what had come before me, whether it was in a sphere biased against women or not. Summarily discarding their work would not eliminate the gap in my education as a writer, I decided.

Despite misgivings outside the scope of this essay, I would like to accept the invitation to have my voice heard in the UK, as a Turkish writer based in Wales, but only on my terms. The literary merits of my work should be separate from and not affected by my refusal to be steered by diversity quota-orientated curators with their own unexamined orientalist tendencies. Furthermore, I want to cleave myself from the clichéd idea that 'Western values' such as freedom of expression and human rights are exclusive to the Occident – there are plenty of indigenous civil society players and activists fighting for progress in Turkey and they are not by any stretch all NGO's and foreign-led or influenced efforts. As a counterweight to the argument that the West promotes freedom of expression no matter what, I have experienced forms of, albeit rather sophisticated, censorship that I have often baulked at in my screen and novel writing practices in the UK, a country that advertises itself as a bulwark for free speech. I have witnessed first-hand in Wales, for example, how fellow Turkish artists have been induced to pandering to occidental expectations of storytelling with a concomitant craving for exoticism. We are encouraged, I would argue, to produce palatable cultural artefacts for a post-colonial UK marketplace that offers to sustain us in return for a tacit understanding that we turn our backs on our homeland in a way that the British would never countenance for their own artist-citizens at home or abroad.

When I was a teenager, Turkey had become more of an annual holiday destination and pilgrimage to see relatives rather than my actual home. Many terrible things had happened in the eighties just after we left for the UK, including the torture of my uncle by the military regime, thus the disinclination to return to Turkey. It seemed to be a country that was not advancing towards European ideals as envisaged by our illustrious founding fathers. This cemented my concept of Turkey as a struggling nation trying to find its place on the globe and my sister and I, analogously, were busy dealing with the challenges of finding our places in the UK. We were harassed by xenophobic bullies and a wider undercurrent of racism that could only be evaded once we kept our heads down and became more British than the natives. Our changing personalities did not go unnoticed in Turkey where childhood friends and family members remarked that I, for example, had become 'cold and reserved like the English'! Were they projecting this persona onto me based on their own limited knowledge the British people or was it true? In contrast, many of my British peers stated that I couldn't really be a Turk – their evidence, I assumed, being my blue eyes, English accent and paler-than-they-imagined-a-Turk-to-be skin. However, I now know that they had in their mind an engrained image of the Turk, in appearance *as well as in manner*, that I was somehow failing to match. At the time, I rejected the idea that there was such a thing as outright racism towards Turks but I have been disabused of that notion chiefly in light of recent events where the immigrant has been demonised overall and the Turkish nation targeted in particular during the Leave campaign of 2016. Like Turkey itself, I was torn between the East and the West – an appalling dichotomy for an adolescent in the throes of establishing a basic sense of identity. It may be that, trapped in such a dilemma, I was pulled one way by patriotic zeal inherited from my mother's side and pulled another by the ambivalence of being in Turkey exhibited by my father who had come from a small town that he had striven to escape and had found the fulfilment of personal success in a foreign land. He admired the famed Great British know-how and his personality sat well with the notorious British sense of reserve. Though he had not eschewed his cultural roots entirely, he had only allowed us a glimpse of what he knew, offering up his lines of poetry and song as tantalising and, to me, mysterious (I was guilty of exoticising my own culture as part of my self-othering) relics from another reality that his children need not be a part of anymore. By the time I graduated from university in Canterbury, I was nothing more than an ersatz European – a young man who had forgotten he was Turkish (I even shot a short film about it, perfectly oblivious that I was making a film about myself). By not attempting to know myself more fully, to acknowledge the issues of identity that were impeding my creativity because I was afraid of being othered, I had – with delicious irony – othered myself.

Perhaps it is due to all of this retrospective speculation that I found myself standing in a Turkish bookshop with an armful of books thinking that I have betrayed my culture and must make amends so as to complete myself as a human being and a writer. It felt right that I explore my inherited traditions as part of a wider literary education that transcended the Eurocentric. In this way, I could enrich my critical thinking and sense of existing in the world, without intervention from the dynamics of privileged power positions that are inherent when one posits that there is a construct called the Other. To be steered by the dominant culture, oh-so-very subtly and ingeniously so that the interventions are hard to pin down and so impossible to call out, is to be asked to choose a side. When you realise that there are no 'sides' within a person – only cultural paradigms that threaten to compartmentalise a person's psyche and affect their creative output in a damaging fashion – you can aspire to write authentically, with sincerity and authority. You can write directly about your own unique experiences on this planet as a human being, or channel those experiences to inform your practice – whether it be poetry, screenwriting or prose.

The balancing act required of BAME practitioners, it seems to me, is about not equivocating the dilemma of the cultural steering that I propose is going on. Although imposed externally at first, it can then become internalised if not scrutinized when detected. The impact of this on one's work ought to be acknowledged – even embraced – with calm introspection and subsequently resisted if necessary but without further alienating oneself from the realities of the creative industries; keeping the gatekeepers onside is a crucial component of an artist's praxis as an inferior category of suffering. Without access to distribution networks your work may not be visible. Only by unravelling the self-othering that occurs as an active dialogue between the practitioner and the cultural gatekeepers can there be any hope of true freedom of expression without fear of stigmatisation of any kind, and that outcome can only serve to increase the freedom of speech – in its positive forms – that as humans I believe we all seek.

What is boccia? Don't ask me, I just play it

Ricky Stevenson

When I tell people I play a sport featured in the Paralympics, they're impressed. When I simply tell them I play boccia, they stare blankly into my eyes, then ask that dreaded question: 'What's boccia?'

My lips go numb and my brain shuts down.

'What *is* boccia?' I ponder, as if I've been asked to give the exact measurements of the universe, add them up and divide by Pi.

This is what happened when a BBC reporter interviewed me in the run up to the 2018 Boccia World Championships. I knew the question was coming and I knew I'd fail spectacularly at answering it. The reporter never let on that I was rambling, but beneath his permanent grin, his wide eyes and rapid nods, I could tell he wished he'd never asked.

'You have six balls and a jack... Have you ever watched Bowls? It's kind of similar but not really because the balls aren't bowls, and so they run much more like balls than bowls, if you know what I mean....'

Obviously when they aired the piece they cut this bit out, along with the majority of my other nonsense. I'm just a newbie after all – although I've been casually practicing boccia for around eight years, I've only recently joined Team GB as part of their transition squad. More experienced players are so well versed and fed up with answering this question that they carry around pre-prepared sticky notes covering the basics, to be flung at any inquirers (turns out the ability to throw objects with speed and accuracy has real-world uses too).

The question is naturally common since boccia remains an overlooked sport, so much so that perhaps it's a good sign that people are asking questions at all. The best coverage boccia has received so far happened at the 2018 World Championships, where a generous selection of matches was streamed live on the BBC website and uploaded onto YouTube. No live streams were available during the London and Rio Paralympic Games, so I had to settle for watching dressage instead. I have nothing against dressage, but I promise that boccia is far, far easier to grasp than whatever dressage is. And I'm sure I'm not the only one who thinks this. Why don't BBC reporters ask dressage competitors what *their* sport is?

Perhaps one reason I'm reluctant to provide an easy answer to the question is because I don't want to undermine how bloody hard it is. Football is just a matter of passing a ball around until you're close enough to kick it into a massive net. Easy, right? Well in boccia you simply have to make sure that you throw all your balls closer to the jack than your opponent… except both you and your opponent have a physical disability which has a considerable impact on both your dexterity and throwing ability.

In boccia there are four categories of players including BC3s, for example, who use a ramp from which they launch their balls and require an assistant to manoeuvre it under their instruction. But I can only speak as a BC1 (someone affected by cerebral palsy) and as a BC1 you can never be sure where your balls will end up. You have good days and bad days, but for me boccia feels generally like playing darts with a shaky hand (I'd imagine – I wouldn't dare throw a dart. Even if I was in the middle of the Sahara Desert, I know I'd end up killing something or else stabbing my own eye out.)

Nevertheless, during the 2017 Boccia UK Championships, I inexplicably played my best boccia to date and was very lucky that coaches from Team GB were there to see it. I was apparently good enough to land a spot in the team's transition squad, in which players are selected for their potential to reach an elite level. That was over a year ago, when I was naive to the fact that I had a lot of work to do, work which would seemingly never end.

The two-day competition passed by like a nice fluffy dream. My throws were accurate, my technique solid throughout, and at no point did I put anyone's life in danger via wayward throws (a major achievement in itself). I learned first-hand what it means to be in 'the zone', and when I received my Silver Medal I couldn't believe it. My biggest highlight was a tight game against the top-ranked BC1 in the world. What on earth had happened? It didn't make sense. For the past three years, he'd hammered me and I'd treated this competition as a bit of demented fun, exiting at the group stage each time. Now, over the course of two days everything had changed: I'd discovered that, when playing at my best, I could be a threat to anyone.

Yes, gone were the days of intimidating only the referees who stood too close or anyone unfortunate enough to be fixing the ceiling lights during one of my matches. Now I possessed something called ambition and another thing called confidence and these would continue to grow throughout the transition camps as I established myself as a skilled and consistent player. Then in March 2018 I took part in my first international competition for Team GB: the Bisfed 2018 Madrid Regional Open. Time to make my mark!

Sitting in the waiting room opposite my first opponent of the day, I was pumped. I searched his eyes for weakness. I assessed his body for weakness too. In high-level boccia the nurturing attitude that tends to surround disabled people is turned upside down. In the arena of sport and competition, disability is seen as something to exploit. If I clock that my opponent has a weak arm, for example, it can leverage confidence that I'll beat them since my strong arm is an advantage. Nobody feels sorry for anyone here – not during a match anyway.

Back in the waiting room, my time had arrived. I was going to rock up to that court, land my first ball straight onto the jack and stroll towards thunderous victory! And I lost, heavily: 11-0. *Ouch.* I entered the next match shell-shocked but desperately optimistic. Final score: 12-0 to my opponent. My biggest defeat at the UK Championships was 5-1 and that was against the World No.1. What had changed since then? What had changed since last week in training when I was still throwing with a sense of ease and flourish? Here in Madrid every shot felt stiff and unnatural, each match a grind. My third and final Individuals match was far closer – I lost by just a point – but I left the court with a sense of unease. I hadn't performed the way I wanted to and 'the zone' had completely deserted me. But my mood would U-turn two days later when the BC1/BC2 Team I played substitute for won Gold! After all the turmoil and torment of the Individuals, I was now a Gold Medalist… welcome to elite boccia, everyone, a world where you never know what's around the corner.

While teamwork is important, for the sake of simplicity

(and self-indulgence) let's keep the focus on my experiences as an Individual BC1 player. My road to the Boccia World Championships 2018 in Liverpool was bumpy to say the least. Apart from a hard-fought win during the Bisfed 2018 Povoa World Open, I remained displeased with my performances. The 2018 UK Championships were staged in June, a month prior to the main event. Here was my chance to reignite the passion and confidence I'd experienced just under a year ago! If I hoped to make a dent on the world stage, I needed to prove to myself that I remained the second best BC1 in Britain – that I was worthy of the incredible privilege that lay ahead of me in Liverpool. Would I succeed?

Well… no. I was knocked out at the group stage, a complete one-eighty to last year's competition. What on earth had happened? Would I ever experience 'the zone' again? I had to put the competition (and questions) behind me and move my attention onto the World Championships. I faced a tough group due to my low ranking, but I took this as a positive: I was the underdog again and my only goal was to put my experienced opponents to the test. And I did, in a way. I won an end in each match and made one player in particular sweat under pressure. But winning was never on my mind here – my opponents were just too good and I felt frankly outclassed. *If only I could've provoked that sense of flow and confidence I'd once experienced…* I paused the thought and remembered my goal. One of my opponents later reached the final so I couldn't have played too badly.

I had tried my best in Liverpool but the fact is – in sport – there's a big difference between trying your best and playing your best. Over the past year I've been regularly documenting my feelings, experiences and reflections on my journey as a transition player for Team GB. Below are excerpts from a selection of entries I wrote during a recent training camp in

February, which centered around a competition. I'm returning to it here in the hope that it will offer up a sense of my current feelings towards boccia and maybe it will even help answer the question for myself: what is boccia?

Day 1:

I have little confidence about the competition tomorrow. In the recent UK Championships I lost to people I used to beat consistently and, unfortunately, a few of them have turned up here. Tonight I'm sleeping in a different building than usual, an old jail that's been renovated; the bars have been removed and the blood scrubbed off the walls. Hey, as long as I have a toilet and shower I can fit into, I'm happy. It's a learned happiness that comes from travelling with the team to a hotel with just one accessible shower room to be shared amongst us, and where the lifts were so tight you'd be lucky to fit one wheelchair in; not fun with the hotel accommodating at least ten teams of athletes.

Day 2:

I played two matches today, lost both by some distance. Scores can be harsh in boccia. I try to ignore them. You can lose 9-0 because of one bad round out of four.

Day 3:

I lost two more games today. Although losing to the World Champion is to be expected, a player I would once dominate also beats me convincingly. He's improved so much I'm left wondering if there's any improvement left in me. It seems the more you chase 'the zone', the more it eludes you.

One thing that hasn't helped is that my medication was changed a week ago, leaving me feeling less in control of my body than usual. Matches are usually tiring but these past few days I've been in more of a battle with my body than with any of my opponents.

Day 4:

Today I spent an hour or two with my coach doing a repeti
exercise which was both educational and a challenge in abstain
from ripping your stupid boccia balls apart because 70% of th
don't land where you want them. My main weakness is my m
strength: power. My strong arm is useful for blasting balls to
back of the court but less reliable for the short game. If I was a gol
I imagine I'd happily whack the ball over a load of trees, but as so
as I'd see the hole up close I'd probably start shaking.

So, what is boccia? Part of me gets a sick satisfaction from tl
fact that I'm a marginalised voice practicing a largely ignore
sport. It's now obvious to me why veteran players despi
being asked what this little boccia thing is all about. The
devote all their time and energy into the sport, win meda
for their country, go through all the emotional ups and dowr
as in any other sport, and yet outside the camps, competition
and training sessions, one simple question can make it al
seem a bit irrelevant. So next time I'm asked, 'What's boccia?
My answer will be, 'Decide for yourself.'

Crisp

Bethan Jones-Arthur

If there's a thing I've learned in my quarter of a century on this planet, it's that Sourz apple taste around about the same coming up as they do going down.

Another thing I've learned is advocating vocally and passionately for LGBTQ+ rights and then *vehemently* denying you're part of that demographic might tip some people off that you're bisexual.

Yet *another* thing I've learned is that if that doesn't let your mother know about your sexuality, your total obsession with Baby Spice definitely will.

These are all valuable lessons I had to learn before I could say, at the grand old age of 25, that I sort of know who I am and I think I know what I'm doing. But I stumbled a bit on the way.

I stumbled through awkward half-kisses with girls at sleepovers (was it just my school where all the girls said they were bi? I swear we had some sort of queer uprising at the age of 13, where the girls too mature and interesting for the boys in our year escaped the cloud of BO and Lynx Africa to emerge, all open-minded and that, to update their Bebo profiles and declare they'd do both Pete Wentz AND Hayley Williams).

I stumbled through my mid to late teens, belatedly realising that I did like men *and* women, I just needed to stop going out with men who idolised David Cameron (yeah, I can never buy a 'Never Shagged a Tory' top and it's my worst regret) and women who didn't believe in liking both and thought I was a slut, or a cheat, or a closet case. None are true. Well. Any more.

By the time I tripped headfirst into my twenties, through no fault of anyone but myself, I was stumbling away from me – or at least trying to. I was a bit sick of me, a bit sick of my round, useless body, a bit sick of not liking myself. My stumbling away had led me to an altar of wine bottles; originally two or three, then five or six, then enough to fill two Cardiff Council issued recycling bags which I couldn't get rid of because hauling them down the stairs would mean my uni housemates realising I was sometimes a bit of a big fat wino who liked scoffing cheese puffs and watching Nigella on repeat.

I realise the irony of that, though I think if Nigella did eat cheese puffs they'd be made with *voluptuous* golden puffed corn, *lusciously* enveloped in delicate slivers of edam and gruyere with *seductive* lashings of parmesan and *sultry* bites of garlic infused camembert. And yes, she'd come down in her negligee to munch them at midnight. Pure filth.

I stumbled home to the Valleys and to Mam. She'd sort me out.

All I knew was that it felt heavy in my chest, like I'd stuffed cotton wool down my throat. Or swallowed a crisp without chewing it enough. You know the feeling, when you're lying on the sofa scoffing some smoky bacon and then one gets lodged in your gullet, sharp and painful, not budging for hours no matter how much water you drink. That's how it felt.

Sunday club is, in my opinion, one of the finest Valleys traditions. Though it's a bit unfair: the men go to the pub at about 11am while the women make Sunday dinner. They come back half cut to stuff their faces with roasties, then complain on the sofa with a tinny while their wives get ready, replacing gravy with lipstick. It's a time-honoured ritual that ended, for my family at least, with a trek up the hill, lugging sweet and sour chicken balls and enjoying an 'om on the prom' (egg fu yung while staggering home) as we laughed.

I was chuffed when I got to join in, because for a while I was stuck babysitting my little brother for my mam and stepdad to go out. I'd pass the time binge-watching *Friends* and trying to thoroughly convince my brother he was adopted. Not from another family. From Bristol Zoo. At least for a time he'd side eye me suspiciously while ferociously denying that he was a shaved chimp we'd taken in when he was little.

But now I was home for Mothers' Day, so instead of self-medicating with cheap wine that could double for balsamic vinegar and Nigella's perfect stuffing (again, pure filth), I was self-medicating with pints of cider and a jukebox that played nothing post 2003. That is until they rolled out the karaoke machine. If you haven't sung karaoke in a Valleys pub on a Sunday night after drinking Strongbow all day, you haven't lived.

I'd been slumped in the corner after giving what I was sure was a *rousing* rendition of 'Say a Little Prayer', with the great artistic choice of starting two octaves higher than I should have and then continuing to increase the pitch every two lines. Delightful.

Auntie Cath was up now, having decided it was absolutely necessary that the whole of the village hear her version of 'Alone' by Heart, but at half the speed. I wasn't sure it was even possible for that song to be any slower, but by God, Auntie Cath had proven me wrong.

'I heeear the tiiiickiiiing of the cloooock I'm lyyyying heeeere the rooom's piiiiitch daaaark'

Mam plonked a lager dash in front of me. It seemed an absolutely wonderful idea to drink it, even though I'd been on cider all day. Lovely.

'Alright love?'

Auntie Cath had been building up to the chorus for a good while.

'Tiiiill nooooow I always got byyyyy on my oooown, I never really caaaared until I met yooooou'

She sat down next to me and put her arm around me. I put my head on her shoulder and smiled dopily, then realised I was smiling dopily so tried to straighten my face so she didn't know I was drunk.

She knew I was drunk. I took a big gulp of my pint.

'I was gonna get a bottle of red, but it's Blossom Hill and Knotty[39] has been keeping it in the fridge again.'

'But the seeeeecret is still my oooooown and my looooove for yooooou is still uuuunknooooown'

Knotty was the landlord. He was called Knotty because he couldn't tie his tie for a rugby presentation when he was fifteen, so he just tied it in a knot. He was 52, but the nickname had stayed.

I think it's a bit of a trend in small villages, especially in Wales. Some of the names in our village were like:

Jimmy Shoes, because one time he lost his shoes on a stag do;

Heinz, whose real name is Dai John, but he has a can of Heinz tomato soup every morning so he was re-christened;

---

[39] All names in this essay are fake because the real nicknames are too ridiculous.

Dai John, who isn't related to the real Dai John, but he looks like he could be;

Arms, because he has long arms;

Debbie Dai, because she's fake Dai John's sister (no relation to real Dai John);

And Gene, who once wore a purple blazer to a wedding and looked a little bit like Gene Wilder in *Willy Wonka and the Chocolate Factory*.

'Tiiiill nooooow I always got byyyyy on my oooown, I never really caaaared until I met yooooou'

'Worra dick.'

Turned out I was slurring a bit now. And frowning, because I was trying not to smile like a fool. Quick, let's have another few gulps of this pint.

It suddenly dawned on me that this was the time.

'Mam.'

'Hooooow doooo I geeeeeet yoooou aloooone'

This was the moment I'd been waiting for. God, I felt a bit sick with nerves.

'Mam, how much do you love me?'

This was when I should come out. The moment was so right. We were there: in a pub that smelled of fag ash and stale ale, surrounded by drunks, and I could feel the words rushing up, begging to come out. This was the time. I downed the last bit of my pint.

'Mam. Listen. S'important. Lissentome. What would you do if I was gay? Or bi?'

She looked at me and wiped a bit of lager from my chin. God, I'm a classy bird.

'I know you like both, love. I've known for a while.'

She patted my knee.

'Alooooooooooooooone'

'I love you. Do you know that?'

'Yeah. Love you, Mam. I'm just gonna get some crisps.'

Well bloody hell, that was easy! I heaved myself up, set on a packet of cheese and onion to line my stomach, and the minute I did all of the cider and lager and apple sourz (don't ask) sloshed around in my system and immediately tried to escape.

Oh no. Maybe I wasn't sick with nerves.

I have never moved so quick in my life. I sprinted to the toilet, past the 'NO DRUGS' posters, past the couple with their tongues down each other's throats, past the wide-eyed group of 'lads' who had very clearly flouted the no drugs rule, and made it just in time to throw up ten pints, a round of shots, and a chip I stole from my brother's plate at lunchtime.

'Aloooooooooooooooooooooone'

My stepfather was right. I should have eaten more earlier. He always says that when you go on an all-dayer, you should eat when you can, like they do in the SAS.

My stepfather has never been in the SAS, but I trust him.

I stepped out of the toilet to hear my Mam singing the first lines of 'Calon Lan'.

All was right with the world as I swayed over to the bar, feeling decidedly stable for someone who was just sick out of her nose.

'Can I have a lager dash and a pack of cheese and onion please?'

I stumbled back to my seat. I felt lighter.

Mzungu

Sarah Younan

Mzungu
/(ə)mˈzʊŋɡʊ/
noun
(in East Africa) a white person

I was born in Germany. I am of mixed European and Middle Eastern heritage. We moved to Kenya when I was nine. We moved to Nakuru, a small town next to a lake full of flamingos. I didn't speak a word of English or Swahili. My first foray into the neighbourhood wasn't much of a success. When you're little, you head out and look for friends. Children can be awful when you look different though. The neighbourhood kids pointed and laughed. They shouted *'Mzungu! Mzungu! Mzungu!'*[40] I remember a parent storming into the small yard, grabbing a kid and whipping him. There was much running around and screaming. I'd learned a new word; *'mzungu'* had permanently entered into my vocabulary via children's voices, laughter and the sound of whipping and screams.

---

[40] 'White person' in Swahili. Possibly from the verb *zunguka* to go around. Because those early colonialists got lost, had heatstrokes, walked in circles. It's not a friendly term, but it's funny.

We enrolled in a local school in Nakuru. Apart from my two sisters and myself, there were only two more *mzungus* in the school; kids of British missionaries. Even though Kenyans tend to be quite religious, you still find a lot of missionaries there. I guess it's easier to save souls in a warm country where people have a lot of faith and respect for the church, rather than being showered with rain and rejection while dragging yourself from door to door in the UK. It's a funny thing though, these Bible people running around, preaching the gospel of white Jesus. See colonialism is over, but some things linger. A religion imposed during colonial suppression, an outdated school system that teaches more about European history than the Mau Mau uprising, a corrupt political structure built on the remnants of an apparatus put in place to strengthen British control, courtrooms still filled with judges sweating under powdered wigs; stale aftertaste of empire. Our first Christmas in Nakuru, I was Mary in the school's nativity play, the missionary boy was Joseph and our siblings were the three wise men. It was our teachers, who were all Kenyan, who put together this strange nativity line up. See colonialism is over, but white Jesus chased out the ancestors and the missionaries keep coming in droves to make sure they don't return. Spreading the word, teaching the heathens, engrained colourism, erasure of heritage, Hallelujah!

My best friend at school was called Angela. She took me home to meet her family. For religious reasons, they weren't eating any animal products. They made a fuss about their *mzungu* guest and insisted that instead of sharing their beans, I ate a huge big omelette and white bread. The family sat silently and watched me eat. Then they filled another plate. It was a really hot day. Stuffed, sweating and uncomfortable, I sat at the table in front of Angela's family and forced down this second mountain of fried egg. See, I was raised to be polite. *'Ngai',*[41] they must have thought; 'these *mzungus* really eat a lot. They must be very hungry.' I remember afterwards, we went for a walk through the market place. Angela noticed that I had my T-shirt on backwards. I wanted to turn it around but she stopped me, horrified; 'Everyone is looking!'

It was okay though. You'd get laughed at, pointed out and stared at, constantly living on an exposed platform. But kids are kids and eventually we'd end up chasing each other, playing football, gossiping about boys by the trees in the schoolyard. Nakuru was sleepy and safe. The locusts came one day and ate all the grass on the football pitch, then they left again. Angela grew breasts and the boys would giggle and stare at her too. Then Baba got a new job in Nairobi with a German NGO, and they offered to cover our school fees at the German School Nairobi, so we moved again.

Nairobi is big; sprawling leafy compounds, even more sprawling slums, and everything in between. Supermarkets, shopping malls, UN headquarters, embassies, hotels, courts, butcheries, markets, street vendors, bus stations, pastoralists herding their livestock on by the roadside during dry season, street kids sniffing glue, hustlers. You never used to see them walking around, but there were plenty of *mzungus* too in Nairobi. Enough *mzungus* to create their own expat circles. See if you come to the West from elsewhere, you're a migrant. As a migrant, you better stop dressing funny, eating funny, looking and smelling funny. Don't hang with those other migrants in that way, with your funny ways, smells, foods and clothes. Integrate! Learn how to 'act normal'!

That doesn't apply to *mzungus* though. They are 'expats' when they move to foreign countries, not migrants. They are

---

[41] 'God' surprised exclamation, Swahili.

called NGO workers, consultants, reporters, diplomats, hoteliers, safari tour operators and development workers; noble and adventurous folk who consider themselves citizens of the world. See if you're a 'citizen of the world', there's no need to integrate; you can sip your imported chilled beverage in an expat hangout, where everyone is tanned, worldly-wise and weary. There, you can bond over stories about your adventures in these foreign parts, of how nothing works and the people are corrupt, untrustworthy, underqualified and childish. In expat circles, no one will mention your embarrassing lack of melanin, comment on your accent or question your right to be here. The word *mzungu* will not be shouted at you. As an expat, you live in a country, but you're not in it.

My new German School was full of little expat kids. Kids with German accents, many with well-off parents. They lived in big houses with big gardens and pools behind big fences and spent their afternoons in shopping malls. Suddenly surrounded by other *mzungus*, new tribal lines and distinctions came into play. Suddenly, I wasn't quite German enough. No one shouted *'mzungu'* at school anymore, but I gained new names; 'Pube-head! Potato-nose!' It wasn't until years later that I realised those were my ethnic features; big nose, curly dark hair. I wasn't quite *mzungu* enough after all, at least not to those kids. This came as a relief.

Puberty hit, and new social opportunities opened up outside of school. By social opportunities, I mean older guys who'd buy me drinks and take me out. By the time I was 16, my parents were busy skipping town to avoid having to deal with their bombed-out marriage and each other. No one kept check on how I came and went at home. Every night, the city would roll over and expose its underbelly. Suddenly, the social bubbles that kept people apart during the day would pop and we would morph into a hungry night crowd, looking for music, alcohol and sex. *Yani*,[42] if you throw yourself into Nairobi at night, someone will catch you.

I started looking down on my classmates and their tame teenage adventures fondling each other at private parties in big houses behind big fences. I'd be in town. I'd be out-out. The bullies no longer scared me, I knew what their parents got up to. 'Hey, I saw your dad in the club feeling up on the *malayas*'.[43] The world was broken, intimacy and morals were a lie and you couldn't tell me fairy tales.

If they stayed in Nairobi and didn't head straight to the coast or another national park, tourists would go to feed the giraffes at Nairobi National Park. They would go to Maasai Market to buy curious, to Carnivore Restaurant to eat grilled crocodile and ostrich and gazelle, and to Karen Blixen Museum, named after that colonial baroness with the gaunt face who had a 'love for Africa'. Mind you, it wouldn't have been too much love. The baroness was colonial thoroughbred and did things the proper White African way: 'don't go native darling, they all have AIDS'. She only loved *mzungu* men who all went on to die tragically in the bush some way or another. And then she did the right thing again and wrote a book about it, all longing and African sunsets and lions and decorative backdrop savages who chase cows and make a mess of scrambled eggs or whatever.

Anyway, Karen is also the part of Nairobi where many of Kenya's post-colonial white farmer types keep a second city-home. Nice houses, walled compounds with large gardens and bored *mzungu* housewives with too much bohemian silver jewellery on their fingers and wrists, all married to the

---

[42] 'I think'/'you see' in Swahili.

[43] *Malaya* – lady of negotiable affection.

118

kind of husbands who worship Hemmingway, speak in grunts and have big, sunburned, freckled arms. The wives have that leathery look too, wear flowing clothes and tussled hair, they drive four-by-fours. They have farms, they run safaris, and there is that cousin in Zambia who is a big game hunter. Born and bred, living and breathing Africa, 'but just the landscape and animals dear, don't mix with the *watu*[44]'; that's something the tourists do, not the born and bred.

I was out on a weeknight in a bar in Karen when I met a tourist lady. Let's call her Sabina. Karen wasn't a typical spot, but the guys had wanted to go *mzungu* chasing. Bonyface, who we called 'Pickup' was our designated driver, which never stopped him drinking.[45] He thought the nickname was because he was good at picking up chicks but really, he had no grace and we were using him for his battered Toyota pickup – no one else had a ride. Everything was a hustle, including our friendship; it was easier to score a *mzungu* chick if you already had one on your team. It made the tourists feel at ease.

Sabina was in her late twenties. She told us how she'd spent three months in a village to finish her SOAS anthropology course with fieldwork. She said she'd truly immersed herself in the culture of the Maasai people. Really loved it. So much so she now sported a head full of dreadlocks, Maasai bead necklaces, a peeling nose, a head wrap and a waist wrap, copper bangles on her arms, and a husband-to-be. A real Maasai, it was authentic, it was African, it was love! His family had sung and danced and cooked a goat and now she too was a Maasai woman, a real Mama

---

[44] 'The people' in Swahili, often derogatory use to refer to 'common' Kenyans by white Africans.

[45] Why bother when you can easily pay off the police?

Africa. Things a degree in anthropology can get you. The guys at the table humoured her, scoping out if there were any more ladies with yellow hair that were interested in an ethnography degree.

Sabina and her authentic Maasai husband were only in Nairobi for the weekend, and she asked if we could show them around. They also hadn't booked a hotel yet, and asked if we could recommend somewhere that wasn't as expensive as Karen. Sabina asked for somewhere 'more authentic'. We decided to head to this joint in Kileleshwa, where you could get good *nyama choma*[46] and cheap drinks and the owner even had rooms for rent (usually at an hourly rate).

The place in Kileleshwa was a converted villa, former bedrooms filled with plastic chairs and tables, corrugated iron huts that spill into the garden. There was a big barbecue pit in the courtyard and pots of hot oil. Goat, cow and pig carcasses hung in the garage. Boniface went to choose the meat and we sat in a hut close to the bar while the chef roasted our goat. Sabina got one of the hourly-rate rooms upstairs and dropped off her bags. Ndombolo, Lingalla and Dancehall was crackling from the speakers. The sun had set but it was still warm. The joint filled up and became lively with smoke, warm beer, armpits, roasted meat, sticky skin on plastic furniture. Sabina looked washed out in the blue fairy lights strung up under the corrugated-iron roof of the hut. Those Maasai beads were not a good contrast with her skin. She talked a lot in a funny British accent we all had trouble understanding, mostly about her time in the village and how it had all just been so real. 'Authentic' seemed to be her favourite word.

I couldn't stand her. The vanity of small differences; I was

---

[46] Grilled or fried meats.

a *mzungu, sawa*,[47] but I never wanted to be THAT kind of *mzungu*. Not like those born-and-bred white Africans; not the pretentious expat types, not the clueless tourists, and certainly not a 'white Maasai'. Sabina had so much assurance, not a hint of doubt; she *knew* she belonged there. It's harder to fool yourself in Nairobi. Nairobi is many things, but it is not a city for romance or dreams of an unspoilt Africa.

People started dancing by the bar and between the tables. Sabina stayed firmly planted as the women twerked, men watching them, couples grinding together. Mama Africa shrunk back into a plastic seat, side eyeing her husband as bodies around her moved. Authentic Maasai husband was feeling the beer and the music and trying to coax her 'come dance *mpenzi*[48] life is short' but Mama Africa reported a headache and went to lie down in her hourly-rate room with the aircon on. We continued to dance and drink. Authentic Maasai husband bought a bottle of Kibao.[49] I danced with him that night.

Maybe in her room upstairs, with the AC on and finally sleeping despite the heat, the stale sheets and the noise downstairs, Sabina dreamt of a journey to the most remote and mysterious corners of the world, a place with unspoilt wilderness. Maybe she dreamt she met a real warrior and joined his tribe. Perhaps she saw the Great Rift Valley in her dream. Maasai herding cattle through the bush, and she marvelled at their traditional way of life. Maybe she dreamt she was one of them.

There's no moral here. By all means, go on a safari and

---

[47] 'okay' or 'alright' in Swahili.

[48] darling.

[49] Kenyan spirit, tastes like the bastard child of gin and vodka.

121

feed some giraffes. Go visit the Karen Blixen Museum, or go to the coast where beach boys will offer you coconuts and anything your heart desires. Go have an 'adventure'. Go chase whatever dream of Africa you have – Kenya is a hospitable nation and *mzungus* are much loved. Al Shabab's attacks have destroyed the tourism industry, so go see dancing Maasai warriors, photograph wild animals and eat some crocodile. And if you're more into the Bono brand of Africa then there are wells to be dug, souls to be saved, orphans to be hugged. So go and save a child or two and take a Facebook profile picture while you're at it. Go donate your second-hand clothes to some slum dwellers in Kibera and then go back home and tell people about your deeds.

What you say goes. You're the colour of Jesus, you're the three wise men; you come bearing gifts. You have money to spend and it's your particular African Dream that you will find. Want to save some souls? Go for it. Dig some wells? Go for it. Find a warrior husband? Go for it. Bring your learned SOAS theories, your Hemingway adventures, your tacky romance novel cravings, your conservationist/aid worker/gap year white saviourism. You will find your dream; people will accommodate you, and if the sun burns too hard or if people laugh at you and you can't join in the dance, there will be malls and tour buses and expat hang-outs, smiling attentive waiters and aircons.

> *Mzungu* privilege; the world is shaped around you.
> *Mzungu* underpriviledge; the world is not yours to experience.

Jambo! Jambo bwana[50]
Habari gani? Mzuri sana
Wageni mwakaribishwa
Kenya yetu – Hakuna matata
Kenya nchi nzuri – Hakuna matata
Nchi ya maajabu – Hakuna matata

---

[50] Song sung to tourists in Kenya:
Jambo! Jambo bwana – Hello! Hello sir
Habari gani? Mzuri sana. – How are you? Very fine.
Wageni mwakaribishwa – Visitors are welcome
Kenya yetu, hakuna matata – Our (country) Kenya, (there are) no worries
Kenya nchi nzuri, hakuna matata – Kenya is a nice country, (there are) no worries
Nchi ya maajabu, hakuna matata – A beautiful country, (there are) no worries.

Bipolar Disorder

Dafydd Reeves

The main thing I remember was the pressure and the fear: in a mental hospital surrounded by my parents and the nurses, all urging me to take the medication.

To be fair, they had a very good point. I was extremely distressed and my mind racing with terrifying delusions. This was in part, unfortunately, due to talking with an extremely disturbed person who I shared the ward with. He was interested in the transhumanist movement, a futurist movement that advocates, among other things, melding humans and machines in order to live forever. Ideas of religion, conspiracy and science-fiction, what we might call the fringes of the real, are often the domain of the mentally ill (although of course not all transhumanists are necessarily mentally ill as much as I find their ideas dangerous and repellent.)

In my fragile state, I regarded the person in question as a kind of dark prophet preaching of a terrifying, deathless future populated by cyborgs. What these cyborgs were getting up to, was either hilarious, inane or horrifying depending on your state of mind. I can laugh now, but at the time I was horrified.

A period of mental disturbance had preceded me going to the hospital. I had been having dreams that I was living in a simulation, an idea familiar to anyone who has seen the film *The Matrix*. This is also a key facet of 'Gnostic' religions, something I had been reading about earlier and which may well have coloured my experience. The theme of Gnosticism is something that will appear time and again in this essay.

What did my dreams involve? I dreamt I was in of a kind of machine realm, populated by pixel-like triangles, like sinister origami birds, that moved and flexed like a kaleidoscope. They had wheedling voices; they reminded me of nasty cosmic nerds, playing games with the universe and everyone in it. It was clear that these were the masters of the simulation, what is known in Gnosticism as 'archons'.

I unwisely told the person in question of this and he replied in a cryptic and deadpan voice, 'ah yes, they are called "crofaxes"'. Now, as I often joke when I tell this anecdote: one person with a delusion is one thing but two people sharing the same delusion is a cult. So when my father outstretched his palm with a pill in his hand, urging me to take the medication, all that was going through my mind was 'this is the red pill. If I take it I will wake up from *The Matrix*'. I thought that if I took the pill the world would be revealed to be an illusion and I would wake up to a terrifying machine hell.

I refused to take it. I said that I just wanted to be left alone. I promised I would stop crying and making noise. Most of all, I begged: 'please don't make me take the pill'. Consequently, I was strongly pinned down by a group of male nurses and a needle was jabbed in my backside. Considering the disturbing images of cyborgs that were placed in my mind earlier, I was particularly vulnerable and completely misinterpreted what was happening. Though I know everybody had my best interests at heart, it was a fairly traumatic experience. This is why I chose to compose a fairy tale as an interpretation of my experience. It goes as follows:

Rhwngdaubegwn was one of the ten princes and princesses of the faeries. Each of them were named for their personality; Gwregys Bregus ('Brittle Belt') was so named for has fat belly and his sense of humour, which burst his belt when he laughed; Diom Bwys ('No Worries') for his easy-going and relaxed demeanour, and Penogymylau ('Head of Clouds') because she was an airy philosopher (just to name a few). Why Welsh names? Because a pure form of Welsh was spoken in the Garden of Eden and the faeries are the children of Lilith, the first wife of Adam.

Rhwngdaubegwn in particular was aptly named as his name meant 'between two polarities'. He was a bard, with quick wit and a sharp tongue, able to captivate with honeyed verses of enchantment or to deflate with a few withering words of satire. He also suffered from changes in mood; from the most soaring euphoria to the most miserable pits of depression and sometimes a curious blend of the two.

One day, Rhwngdaubegwn stumbled drunkenly into the hall of the faerie royalty at Caerymaros (the Waiting Fort, a limbo between worlds) and fell into an argument with Wfftibopeth ('Arse to Everything') the nihilistic magician. So fierce was the argument that Rhwngdaubegwn leapt on Wfftibopeth and assaulted him furious blows which did not stop as he fell to the floor. The faerie royalty restrained him and accosted him. King Lloer Lloyw 'Pale Moon' asked the rest of the faeries, with their combined magic, to create a salve that would subdue Rhwngdaubegwn in his erratic agitation. The rest of the faeries complied and with their combined sorceries produced a magic cactus whose spikes contained a potent serum. Whosoever was pricked in the arse with a spike of the cactus (it had to be the arse for some reason) would be sedated.

And so they collectively pinned Rhwngdaubegwn down and pricked him in the arse with the cactus. Rhwngdaubegwn soon calmed down and turned to his family and said, 'I was not myself, you were right to do what you did'. And for a while that was the end of that.

However, one day Rhwngdaubegwn came into the hall of Caerymaros and was again in a foul mood; frighteningly animated yet utterly despairing. He began hitting himself on the head and screaming and tearing out his hair. The royalty wasted no time in restraining him again, pinning him to the floor and pricking his arse with the cactus. After a while, a calmer Rhwngdaubegwn turned to them and said, 'I was not myself, it might have been right for you to do what you did.'

As common in many of these stories, there came a third time for Rhwngdaubegwn to be in one of his furious moods. He stormed into the hall of Caerymaros and immediately turned his silver tongue to the purpose of spouting the most barbed and baroque insults and most laviscious and loquacious slights to every member of the royalty. He used his guile and perception to discern their most guarded secrets and exploit their deepest insecurities to create as much havoc and misery as possible.

Promptly, the faerie court pinned him down to the ground and pricked him in the arse with the cactus. But this time when Rhwngdaubegwn came to he said 'I was not myself' before adding 'but it was not right for you to do what you did. The first time I was a physical threat to others and the second time I was a threat to myself. However there is no rightful law that can restrain the freedom of the tongue, no matter how vile or provoking the words might be.' The faerie royalty agreed shamefaced that there was indeed no actual law against being an upsetting arsehole and that they had abused their power.

There is a happy ending however, as Rhwngdaubegwn agreed to take a small dose of the cactus serum on a monthly basis to curtail his mood. And from then on there was an understanding between him and the rest of the royalty.

And that's the story. Its basic moral is that the question of forced medication is justified only when a person is a physical threat to others or themselves. I am very libertarian bent in my views here. I don't believe a person should be forcibly medicated for their behaviour simply because it is eccentric or even upsetting to others. After all, 'there's no actual law against being an upsetting arsehole'. However it is one's moral responsibility not to be. Fundamentally this is a question of free speech.

The example I use to illustrate this is Boris Johnson and his infamous comment that veiled Muslim women look like 'letterboxes or bank-robbers'. Undoubtedly offensive, lazy and careless words, particularly from a powerful and highly-visible politician who should know better. In our benighted society, we have the freedom to say or express ourselves in whatever way we choose within reason. However, though you have the freedom to say anything, you have a responsibility not to because your words have consequences, as in Johnson's case where veiled women were openly being jeered in the street for their choice of dress by emboldened plonkers.

In brief, what I'm advocating is responsibility from the individual and non-interference from the state. The idea that the state pinned me down and jabbed me in the arse because I was erratic (something that I couldn't help) was not only regrettable because of my delusional mental state and how it made things worse but also because it was a violation of my human rights. Thus, my little fairy tale is something I truly believe in and am proud of, and as a person interested in the traditional art of oral storytelling, one I hope I can perform to others one day.

Folklore, mythology, fairy tale and religion can often provide insight and shed light on the issue of mental health and inform how we cope with it.

So what's going on in a mind like Rhwngdaubegwn's? The current model we have for bipolar disorder is that it is a condition caused by a chemical imbalance in the brain. I, for one, don't think I buy it. It strikes me as something of a cop-out. *All* brain activity is due to chemicals. The West has a long tradition of focusing on diagnosing (not an accidental word) what is wrong with us and postulating cures.

St Augustine's diagnosis was Original Sin and his cure was Jesus Christ. Another philosopher Thomas Hobbes[51] diagnosed 'rapaciousness' and the cure was rule of law. Freud diagnosed 'neurosis' and the cure was psychoanalysis. Then finally somebody decided that the problem was a chemical imbalance and what was needed was, you guessed it, more chemicals. Do you see the pattern? Each theory is more materialistic than the last.

This very Western way of thinking contrasts with some Eastern philosophies like Taoism, something that I will touch upon shortly. Taoism focuses on what is *right* with us rather than what is wrong with us, namely the innate capacity for harmony. This is why I dismiss talk of chemical imbalances as materialistic, unimaginative and unsatisfactory. In my view, the problem fundamentally is a spiritual one.

---

[51] Marinoff, Lou, 'Thomas Hobbes: A grim portrait of human nature', *TLS* (date unknown).

Spirituality often gets a bad rep these days and I for one often rip into hippy-dippy vague thinking. But for my money, what I define as 'spirituality' are concerns that are non-physical, such as consciousness, something which science can't account for. In my view, a person with bipolar disorder is simply a spirit out of balance. To support my view, I turn to the words 'manic' and 'maniac'. Where do these words come from? I once read a book by Idries Shah called *The Sufis*.[52] Now I have to be very careful what I say here because I do not wish to fall into the trap of Orientalism and mischaracterise Sufism or *tasawwuf* (often described as the spiritual or mystical dimension or Islam), but there was one concept in the book that struck me as being important.

There is a reason some words have the precise meaning that they do. The etymology of words, the sound and shape of them, often contain hidden treasures. In Arabic in particular, they might well alliterate with words which have associative meanings. Or the root of the word might lead you to a deeper wisdom, a deeper understanding.

One of these words is the word 'manic' as in a 'manic episode' or 'manic depression' – a derivative of the word 'maniac'. A 'maniac' in its original sense was a pejorative term for one of the Manicheans, and Manicheanism was one of the Gnostic religions.

The Manicheans, like all Gnostics, were what is called dualists; cosmic dualists to be precise. Dualism is a facet of many religions, not least of which the Abrahamic religions. In Judaism, Christianity and Islam there is God and there is the Devil, but the former is more powerful than the latter which means that one day good will vanquish evil in the event known variously as the apocalypse, Armageddon or the Day of Judgement where

[52] Idries Shah, *The Sufis* (London: IFS Publishing, 1964).

the good go to Heaven and the bad go to Hell. (I hesitate to add this may not reflect the beliefs of all modern monotheists.) This is an example of 'mitigated dualism'.

The Gnostics are different. They are cosmic dualists. They believe that there are two gods, a god of light and a god of darkness and each is equally powerful, meaning that they are fated to wrestle with each other for all eternity. History in this view is cyclical, going around and around in circles. There is no last day and rather than Heaven and Hell, there is reincarnation.

Manicheanism was an example of a Gnostic religion and as such they equated the god of darkness with matter and the god of light with spirit. This is why we get the word Manichean for a black and white worldview. Maybe one would prefer the term 'maniac' or 'manic'. In Manicheanism, the light and the dark are fundamentally at odds with each other, rather than complimenting each other.

And this crucially, would apply to pretty much everyone I have met who was saddled with the label 'bipolar'. Either they veered too far towards the physical and the dynamic or they focus too passively on the mystery of the world. One cannot remain in any such state indefinitely, and what will inevitably happen is that the further the pendulum swings one way, the further it swings back. Sometimes there is a curious state, as in Rhwngdaubegwn's case, where the dynamic energy and the despair intermingle in what is called a 'mixed episode'.

However, there is a philosophy that is the antithesis of the conflicted Gnostic worldview and that is the Eastern religion. Or more precisely: the Eastern philosophy of Taoism. Taoism was founded by Lao Tzu who wrote the Tao Te Ching, an ancient classic of Chinese literature.[53] Taoism is where we get

---

[53] Lao Tzu, *Tao Te Ching: a New English Version by Ursula K. Le Guin* (Boston: Shambhala, 1998).

the idea of yin and yang, not in conflict with each other, but complimenting each other. The yin yang sign crucially has a bit of the black in the white and a bit of white in the black. This principle goes for everything; a balanced man will have feminine aspects and a balanced woman will have masculine aspects. The black and white worldview is reductive and fatal. To veer too much towards materialism or spirituality, light or dark, like in Rhwngdaubegwn's case, can even result in a dangerous admixture of both; this is why left-wing communism and right-wing fascism have so much in common and why so many philosophical 'idealists' and atheists alike believe that we are living in a simulation, which brings us back to the Matrix idea I mentioned earlier. Funnily enough I've heard this being called 'transhuman spirituality'.

I hesitate to say that there's a magic cure for bipolar disorder but I believe that making a conscious decision to stop engaging in black and white (or Manichean) thinking can be of great benefit.

Studying Taoism made me think beyond the label of bipolar disorder. Labels aren't real, they're just a story; a story you tell yourself. For my money the main problem is that the light and dark within you are at odds with each other, which contributes to black and white thinking. However don't think that I'm advocating giving up medication entirely here; that much should be clear from my earlier story. With many people with bipolar disorder the inner conflict is so ingrained that medication is an important check for their mood and to prevent the onset of a psychotic episode. What I'm advocating is a responsible mixture of balanced thinking and dialogue with one's psychiatrist over a long period of time regarding the right medication and way forward. With the right attitude there is hope that one can reduce one's medication or even live without it entirely.

In Taoism, there is light and there is dark, yin and yang, but above it there is the transcendent Tao that flows through all things: the balance. It is analogous (and I'm being deliberately nerdy here) to the Force in *Star Wars* (especially as shown in the excellent *Star Wars Episode VII* but less of that). But I firmly believe it's true. I almost believe it's self-evident. All Tao means is 'Way' and everything in the universe, including the universe itself, has a certain nature and behaves in a certain way. There is an inherent balance or harmony in nature in general and in our nature in particular that everyone can tap into.

For instance, we all know people who are constantly busy though they seem to get nothing done. The opposite of this is the concept of wu-wei, a paradoxical term hard to render into English but meaning something along the lines of 'active non-action' or 'do-without-doing': Just going with the flow.

This I believe is the meaning of what we call mindfulness. It's probably a very bad translation from Eastern languages. The '-full' bit in mindfulness trips a lot of people up. It's actually a mixture, in my view, of the words 'mind' and 'careful' rather than filling up your mind. Indeed, when one is mindful, one is fully engrossed in a task and the story or 'label' of one's ego, one's self, dissipates away. You become the action. Very Jedi if I may say so.

I want to finish on two final points. One is that we live in a very bipolar or dualist age. There is something that I've heard called the 'California ideology'[54] which seems to think by simply connecting people and creating more technology we can create a utopian society. This is folly. For every light there is dark, and it's safe to say the internet has brought with

[54]Morten Tollbol, 'United States of America: Homeland of The Matrix Conspiracy' (date unknown), mortentolboll.weebly.com.

it a whole host of problems; from the rise of populism, fake news and conspiracy theory, to radicalisation, to unmitigated access to pornography. Social media has its benefits, but it certainly has its ills as well. People post perfect pictures and statuses of themselves, giving an edited version of a perfect life. These people are also chasing the light and the positive and unhealthily trying to stamp out the dark. No wonder there are so many people with mental health problems these days; the very nature of the society we live in is bipolar, or to use my preferred term, dualist.

The more I've contemplated this matter, the more I've come to recognise the importance of balance in the world and how one can't have one thing without the other. There can't be light without darkness. There can't be fate without randomness. There can't be matter without spirit. And there jolly well can't be profundity without a bit of silliness.

And on that note I say, may the Tao be with you, always.

The Other Side

Ruqaya Izzidien

They say there's no such thing as coincidence, but to me, it was the ultimate captor. At any other time perhaps I would have escaped those years unscathed. Any other place, and my existence might not have been so undeniably ironic. But that's the burden of coincidence – when conspiracy and synchronicity mark you between their crosshairs, there is no room for what-ifs.

It comes with a quiet price, a background melody of sorts. While your schoolmates, teachers or colleagues concern themselves with the mundanities of life, you must make that extra calculation – will your thoughts, your actions be misconstrued, simply because of their projection of you? You are in the crosshairs, but to them, it is your existence that is loaded.

I could never tell them how much I envied their worries. I remember that time when Ceri asked Anna, as they bounced on my garden trampoline, how she had found jeans that fit her so well. It's often the strange, small things that stun you. It floored me that people could even conceive to think that their jeans should fit them better. At sixteen I should have been thinking about denim and Nokias and the year of parties ahead, but what happened knocked me off-course, and I've been living refracted ever since.

There are things they never teach you about in school. That, for children of colour, there is always a breath held, an ominous expectation, an undercurrent of I-told-you-so. You will never just be a schoolchild, you are the othered child, the foreign child or, in my case, the Iraqi, Muslim child. There is always a caveat in your identity. And no matter how much you achieve, you will never integrate. That's the point of integration; it is unattainable, and designed to keep you at bay.

They don't teach you this at school. But you learn it anyway.

So even if you speak Welsh, or captain your Eisteddfod team, or win ribbons at Sports Day, it doesn't stop them asking you about *your culture*. The truth is, you are never given the chance to explore your identity on your own terms, because they've already decided it for you.

You learn this, yes, but it takes time.

That's how it managed to fester for so long. It's why I didn't recognise it, even when people crossed the street as they saw me, or when they pretended not to know me in public. It was a self-fulfilling prophecy and I was unknowingly participating in my own treachery. My polite compliance brought me nothing but perpetuation. When you laugh along at your own dehumanisation, what are you but the shrinking violet that vindicates their stereotype?

So they called me the good girl and asked me if my family is poor because 'large families are usually poor.' They told me to translate languages I didn't speak, while never neglecting to inform me of my intellectual limits. It came as a surprise, then, that I, of all people, brought hundreds of children out onto the school yard, banging on the railings and chanting for justice. Who would have expected it from a *good little Muslim girl*? It's a phrase that triggered an acid reflux even then, though I didn't yet have the words to deconstruct it.

I no longer spare the bigoted their blushes, or laugh at racist punchlines. My patience is not the sweetener to this pill. If there is any hope of survival, its bitterness must be crushed between their teeth, its chalked shards left to blister, scratch and leech out this blight.

This lesson was lengthy, turbulent, and painfully learnt. And although it began much earlier, with unfiltered seven-year-olds discussing my brown skin, my dirty knees, and my black hair, the Rubicon was crossed on that schoolyard at 16. That was when I began my metamorphosis, my submission to the othering that was thrust upon me.

I stared into the bathroom mirror, unpinning my headscarf. A metre of black polyester; how could something so decidedly boring warrant such misplaced significance? It could have been a blouse, or a skirt, but its unfortunate position on my head meant that it would spend a lifetime in the spotlight. Its background track would deafen each time a passer-by caught sight of me, or during hair-raising science experiments, or when a teacher would ask me to describe my exotic hair for the class. Just don't ever ask anyone to define exotic.

Beneath my scarf was a bandana; a pirate's sigil for a body fighting to separate itself from their image of her. I pulled out a cherry-red crayon, and scrawled two words across my forehead: the physical expression of an identity in flux. Words that seem an inevitability in retrospect, written as much by the school and circumstance as they were by me. Sometimes we do write our own histories, but usually we don't.

When I left the girls' bathroom, my heart punched both terror and victory into the air as my headscarf received stares that, this time, I had invited. I headed to the assembly hall, ready to spread the word, to begin my inadvertent crossing. Two words branding defiance across my forehead: NO WAR.

Two years before, I'd been walking past the chemistry lab to lunch when two boys I didn't know swung the large doors of the science corridor shut. They were wide with reinforced glass panels through which these boys laughed and mocked me. I used to tell myself that they might have picked anyone to trap. That I had just been unlucky, but any Muslim child can describe that vortex in their stomach that tells them exactly why they had been singled out.

The bell rang. The signal to mobilise. We were running down the corridor, jumping the stairs to keep pace. I felt myself being carried along in a wave of students. Maybe there were five, maybe there were 50. It didn't matter much; all I knew was that, in that swell of bodies and feet, I glimpsed acceptance, and I was weightless.

But it takes more than elation to escape gravity, and Miss Rees was nothing if not grave. She stood legs akimbo, her long arms outstretched like double doors. All I could see was the sneer on her face, but time has softened that memory; I think perhaps she was just shocked, desperate. A line of teachers had amassed behind her. I shouldn't have been surprised that they'd uncovered my plan – I did announce it on a microphone. But I was nothing if not adaptable.

'To the tennis courts,' I shouted, and the crowd stopped momentarily before sweeping back up through the school. Miss Rees pranced around us, swinging her doors. Someone should have warned her that the beat of a wave is nothing compared to the unexpected swell of the riptide.

I ducked below her arm and laughter propelled me further, further, further.

Up at the tennis courts, Mr Evans, and Miss Rees tried to fence students off as they darted under elbows and twisted beyond fingertips, putting into practise their best rugby feints. It was a fool's errand. Word of the walkout had spread faster than the time there was a wardrobe malfunction at the school's Eisteddfod rehearsal; students filtered onto the yard in between lessons, at lunchtime, and they even slipped out during classes; excuses that they needed the toilet, nothing but a load of hot air, so to speak.

By lunchtime, Miss Rees and Mr Evans took a well-earned break from trying to crack our spirit. 200 of us had gathered, putting the school art supplies to good use. Peterwell Terrace had never been so raucous, with every third car acquiescing to our self-assured painted banner to 'Honk for peace.' I swiped the railings with my fountain pen as a car passed. Like a final strike of farewell against the strings on a harp. The cars beeped in response, and I was emboldened, powerful, untouchable.

A rare blaze of February sun sustained us; it bolstered our resolve when we were threatened with suspension. I didn't know Kristian well, but I did know that he preferred to dedicate his genius to annoying the teachers rather than improving his grades, which, retrospectively was still an academic achievement of sorts. The air was fresh, hopeful, bursting with the buzz of what could be. Bethan and Dan loosened the silver and green around their necks and tied themselves to the school fencing. Those who didn't follow suit formed a ring and tied their wrists to one another.

I lay back onto the concrete, each of my hands in the laps of friends. A seagull passed in front of the sun and, where I should have felt jubilation, I found an unexpected moment of horror. Somewhere else, another Iraqi schoolgirl would be sinking into this same warmth, looking up at the sun, as a bald eagle passes in front of it, firing its liberation down into her broken, shattered bones.

I sat up and gulped away the singe in my throat. Miss Rees came running, a large inflexible finger pointed at me, like front-wheel drive was pulling along her floaty dress and indignation.

'Where were you on Saturday?'

'What?' I said. I was still thinking of the other me, the one scattered across a bloodied Baghdad street.

'Were you in Carmarthen?' she was shouting now. From the railings and the far end of the courts the crowds were watching.

'No.' I said. *What trouble was I being accused of in Carmarthen? I wasn't even there…*

'And why not?' she said, her tone turning calmer, self-satisfied. 'If you wanted to protest the war you could have gone to the protest in Carmarthen; or is this just a convenient way to get out of school?' If only smug mic drops had been around back then.

'I was in London, Miss.' I paused for melodrama, 'You know, at the million-person protest.' She looked like she had been slapped. Her accusatory finger dropped, and she turned away. And in that moment, I lamented the years I had spent chasing integration. Why did I need acceptance, when I could be this?

'Anyone who doesn't leave right now,' she shouted, 'will be suspended or expelled immediately.'

She didn't mean it, of course. But it worked. It was one of those movie scenes where all it took was for one person to submit for the floodgates to open. I try not to think about those minutes. Instead I remember the small circle of renegades, fists tied, gangly knees bumping.

Mr Evans crouched down beside me.

140

'It'll go on your permanent record. You've never been in trouble before.'

Somebody tell them that I was never their good little Muslim. I was the progeny of wanderers and perseverers, of rebels and warriors.

He tried a different tack.

'Look at these boys,' he nodded at Kristian. 'He's just here to get out of classes, he doesn't care about your war.'

The splintered limbs of my Baghdad twin reached across the ocean to shake hands with this cruel reminder of my otherness, and I began to cry. For who I had been, for my powerlessness and for the truth in his words, too.

It's a sting that stayed with me throughout the last 17 years. That these same classmates, the ones who stayed and even those who did not, who turned into liberal, open-minded adults, still believed in the line separating us and them. As adults, they mourned Charlie Hebdo, but when I opened my laptop after the Christchurch massacre, I was jarred by the Marbella selfies, the drinks with the lads, the cat memes. Like I said, it's the unexpected things that floor you.

Liberalism is most damaging when it's a veneer for prejudice. When your ally lectures you on racism because of that time an Australian made fun of his accent. When she tells you without a trace of irony that your country was better when it was colonised.

Does it matter that we took a stand, small as it was? Because as British taxes paid for the bombs that fell on Iraqi schools, we continued to attend our classes in our small town. What difference is there that you feel bad about something, if it happens anyway? If your act of solidarity is the virtue you signal to deny your bias?

Mr Evans had no idea how his lesson would haunt me over the years, a prophecy repeated with each milestone, ever true, ever poignant.

But it's another lesson that you're slow to learn when you are young, rosy-eyed and trying to drown out the melodies in your head, trying to shake off the target of coincidence. I wanted to believe my classmates were motivated by conviction, so I told myself that Mr Evans was trying to weaken my resolve. I refused to return to class. Instead, we called the local newspaper, who dispatched a journalist to interview us, and in the final period, we dispersed, happy in our victory over the forces that had body-blocked and intimidated us.

When I entered Biology class, a round of applause broke out. My cheeks burned but the mulch and organs and veins of my body leapt with happiness; here was proof that I had done something worthy with my time.

I wish I could say that my protest disarmed the questions, that it left behind a legacy paved in acceptance. But I confess there was a spark, for just a moment, in which I was no longer the school curiosity, with the large family, the mysterious hair; I was a resistor, like my forefathers.

I mourn who I could have been had my identity not been forced upon me. It's an unknown that will never be answered. What would I have done with the freedom to choose? Who could I have been if the politics of my age hadn't been so providential?

But in the game of coincidence, there's no room for what-ifs.

Belonging

Nasia Sarwar-Skuse

So, here you are
too foreign for home
too foreign for here.
Never enough for both.
　　　– Ijeoma Umebinyuo, *Questions for Ada*[55]

In the much loved 1939 movie, *The Wizard of Oz*, Dorothy (played by Judy Garland) clicks her ruby red shoes, closes her eyes and repeats the words 'there is no place like home'. As a child I loved watching this movie and felt a sense of thrill at this scene: she was returning to her home. Even though the world she had adventured in was a colourful one, home was the sepia farm-life with her aunt and uncle, a place with a sense of belonging.

For me, home was Pakistan where I was born, where my grandparents lived. Home was Manchester, where extended family lived, where I was schooled, where I made lifelong friendships with people with whom I have shared joy,

---

[55] Ijeoma Umebinyuo, *Questions for Ada* (CreateSpace Independent Publishing Platform, 2015).

143

sadness and milestones. I moved to Wales in the late 1990s and made my home here. My children were born in Cardiff, which cemented it as the place I call home. But there was always a pull and nostalgia called me to Lahore or to Manchester, but once there Cardiff called me back. When you reach a certain age, you have lived experiences and accept that this pull is to be expected – and makes for a richer life. At least this was my reasoning whenever I felt out of place and longed for the other home, the one in my past.

In late April 2018, on a beautiful spring afternoon, I was racially abused in Cardiff, some 200 yards from my front door. Aside from the initial shock, and once the adrenaline had settled, something else rushed to fill its place: I became overwhelmed with a sense of displacement. A trajectory of thoughts led me to ask myself if the colour of my skin can unpluck me from a place where I have laid down roots; is this place really my home? Where do I belong, how do I find this place of belonging? The incident stirred in me that all too familiar feeling of never being quite enough no matter where I lived.

This feeling of never being quite enough was not new. I came to Britain as a young child who spoke very little English. Other children were intrigued by my skin and language; it was all very innocent but still a sharp reminder that I was different. This difference was celebrated at home as something to be proud of. My mother, a natural storyteller, would regale my siblings and I with stories from her childhood. She was determined that we did not lose our sense of heritage. Her stories were the first I ever heard, stories of one nation not divided where Muslims, Christians, Hindus and Sikhs lived in harmony. She told us stories of golden fields of wheat, the horses she rode and the rivers in which she swam. Sometimes her voice would catch as she

144

remembered the lost friendships that partition brought. My mother would speak of the *jinn* folklore and black magic, creating a world so different from the cold wet Northern city where we had made our home. My father, himself a poet, would enrich our world with the poetry of Ghalib, Mirza, Iqbal and Faiz, reciting verses like they were incantations. Of course, I was too young to understand that my parents were expressing a longing for the home that they had left behind. I would fall asleep dreaming of a vibrant language, rich traditions and everlasting sunshine.

This yearning for a place of no return is a common diasporic experience. In Welsh, *hiraeth* is homesickness, an intense longing or a grief for the lost places of the past. This longing has been examined both in academic studies and also in fictional literature. In Jhumpa Lahiri's wonderful novel *The Namesake* the concept of home is subtly examined. One of the characters, Ashima, misses the motherland (India). She feels that life in America is different and feels a sense of alienation. Lahiri employs the nation-as-home metaphor quite directly. I recall this very sentiment being expressed by my aunts who busied themselves with attempts at recreating the structures of home.

In those early days of being in Britain, I was filled with curiosity about the world. But the world I found myself in wanted to call me a *Paki* or ask me about the food I ate. I didn't have the language then to tell them that different was not wrong. That world wanted to throw bricks through windows whilst brown children watched television, or spray Nazi symbols on walls. I didn't understand why my uncle taped up the letter box at his home each evening. I was confused why my mother would grasp my hand tight and cross over the road at the sight of football supporters.

I attended a very diverse all-girls high school where those

145

of South Asian and Jamaican heritage outnumbered the white girls. Here I found my own diaspora; a mishmash of Pakistani-Jamaican lingo emerged, and life became very much about living in the present moment. My mother displayed her Pakistani hospitality by welcoming my friends from diverse backgrounds – always an extra plate at the table. Somehow, with the backdrop of racism that culminated in the Moss Side riots in Manchester, the Thatcher years and the explosion of the Madchester music scene, we fumbled through it together, scared but determined.

To find myself subjected to racial abuse in 2018 shouldn't really have come as a shock. The post-Brexit Britain we find ourselves in has set the tone for a racialised country, divided by hate and xenophobia. It is reported that there has been a rise in racism and hate crimes since the 2016 referendum.[56] One only need look at the rhetoric about immigrants to get an understanding of how we are perceived. I cannot help but consider the case of the British teenager Shamima Begum who left the country to join ISIS. Whether she was complicit in the atrocities committed by ISIS or groomed is open to debate and indeed should form the basis of a rigorous legal hearing. However, no such legal action has ensued. Instead, when the pregnant Shamima indicated a desire to return home for the sake of her unborn child she was stripped of her British nationality. One justification given by the British state was that she is of Bangladeshi heritage and not being left stateless. However, the Bangladeshi Foreign Minister is quoted as saying that 'We have nothing to do with Shamima Begum. She is not a Bangladeshi citizen... she never applied for Bangladesh citizenship. She

---

[56] 'Brexit 'major influence' in racism and hate crime rise', *BBC News* (20th June 2019).

was born in England and her mother is British'.[57] The double standards are not subtle when we compare the case of Grace Khadijah Dare, a white British convert to Islam who left Britain in 2012 to join ISIS in Syria. To date, no steps have been taken to strip her of her nationality.

I find the insidious climate, where immigrants are perceived to be here in order to take advantage of the system, exhausting. The roots of this sentiment are deeply embedded in colonialism. Britain exported her culture as superior, with the ideas of enlightenment posited as being uniquely European. Britain continues to deny its true colonial violence, and this is evident in the teaching of history in schools. We are taught about the industrial revolution yet this is not coupled with teaching about colonised labour. As such, coloniality which is the legacies of European colonialism, becomes the hangover of colonialism and the lens through which migrants are viewed. It governs our everyday.

I find myself asking: if it were not for colonialism would my parents have migrated? Had it not been for depravation of education at the hands of the British, leaving a society with 16% literacy, a life expectancy of 27, and over 90% living below the poverty line,[58] had it not been for divide and rule, would we be here? I am reminded of the phrase coined by the late Ambalavaner Sivanandan, 'We are here because you were there'.[59] We are here amongst the racism and fear and mistrust, we are here, and we are not going anywhere.

When I encounter difficult situations my response is

---

[57] 'Shamima Begum is not our problem, says Bangladesh government', *Yahoo News UK* (3rd May 2019).

[58] Tharoor, Shashi, '"But what about the railways...?" The myth of Britain's gifts to India', *The Guardian* (8th March 2017).

[59] Speech by the IRR's director, A. Sivanandan, at the IRR's 50th celebration conference 'Catching History on the Wing' (1st November 2008), www.irr.org.uk.

always to work it out on paper. Writing helps me to make sense of things, it empowers me and is a route into self-individualisation. Following the racial abuse, I wrote in order to work through my sense of displacement. I asked myself what home means to me? A hybrid who was born in one country, brought up in another and settled in a third is the product of multiple geographic locations and each border crossed brings a geopolitical experience. I know that this feeling is not unique to me, it's a common diasporic sentiment. I wrote that home is not merely the bricks and mortar we adorn, furnish and fill with love, laughter and dreams – it is also the city that one knows intricately, its geography and history intertwined with one's own. Home is bonded in sounds, smells and moments etched in the mind: lighting fires on cold evenings or the sight of the first snowfall. It is a place where relationships are formed with people and the environment. Home is the house that I share with my family, where I can imagine freely and create without inhibition. Home is where I can shut out the world and envelope myself in my own mythical places. I listed all the geographic places that feel like home. I questioned what it was about those places that felt like home. Was it the location, the people or something else? I considered the language we use to describe ourselves, and how we are described by others. For me, the word immigrant is loaded with the connotation of the lesser, a trespasser and a second class citizen. It feels like a derogatory term assigned to anyone who isn't white European because they have the privilege of calling themselves expats. They are not immigrants. I realised that language and the way it is employed gives us a sense of safety or its polar opposite.

Finally, I arrived at the conclusion that it is within the act of writing that I find my sense of belonging, and in this way

I carry my home with me. On the blank page I can exist in liminal spaces by creating a winter's day strolling along the river Irwell in Salford, or write passages that put me in the whirlwind of festivities in Lahore, or the serenity of an autumnal walk through Bute Park in Cardiff. Writing on the page is the place where I can wander and slip between spaces called home. There is a freedom to this, for I can make my home wherever I go by opening my notebook and grasping my pen. Sometimes you have to leave the place you call home, put a distance between yourself and it, in order to find your way back; this is possible to do on the page.

In my own way I live outside others' expectations of where my home should be, defining my own places of belonging. Home is anywhere that catches my imagination, where language wraps me in its arms and asks me to stay a little longer. The home I build, letter by letter is a place where I live wild and free. But, writing in a language that is not my mother tongue means that others might want to label my work: BAME writer, underrepresented writer, writing about 'our' issues, there might even be an expectation that in order to be accepted as a writer I should write about particular subjects, and frame them in a mainstream manner. But the truth is that I write about things that matter to me. I write to excavate the places which are buried within me: a room in a house from long ago, the scent of my mother's garden or an issue which asks for my attention. Each word I write tells me that I belong.

Contributors

Isabel Adonis was born in London to Welsh and Caribbean parents. She travelled to the Sudan and Nigeria and now lives in north Wales. Her main interests are art, writing and education.

Adonis is currently preparing for an upcoming exhibition in The Weaver's Factory in Uppermill, Greater Manchester. She is also writing a book about race issues and is a private tutor to primary aged children. She is published in *New Welsh Review*, *Urban Welsh*, *Journal of Caribbean Studies*, *Between a Mountain and the Sea*, *Hiraeth*, *Erzolirzoli – A Wales, Cameroon Anthology*. She has a self-published novel called *And, a conjunction of History and Imagination*.

Kate Cleaver is currently studying for her PhD at Swansea University in Creative Writing and History. She is exploring the new field of creative history by researching the lives of twelve patients that found themselves committed to Briton Ferries private insane asylum in the late 1800s. Vernon House was never meant to be an asylum and its history is a turbulent one that ultimately led to its closure and destruction. All that remains of the patients, doctors and the building are ghosts in the historical record. Cleaver is asking if those ghosts can be recreated into stories, into creative history.

Taylor Edmonds is a poet and performer from Barry. She recently completed an MA in Creative Writing at Cardiff University. Her work has been published by *BBC Sesh*, *Wales Arts Review*, *Butcher's Dog Magazine*, *The Cheval Anthology*, *The Cardiff Review* and more. Taylor has worked on projects with The Arts Council of Wales, Nescio Ensemble, The Severn Estuary Partnership and more. Taylor is also a team member of Where I'm Coming From – a Cardiff open mic platforming BAME writers in Wales.

Dylan Huw is an Aberystwyth-born, Cardiff-based writer of fiction, essays and criticism, and a staff member at National Theatre Wales. His particular interests are in writing creatively about and alongside contemporary art, dance and performance, and queer history. He holds an MA in Visual Cultures from Goldsmiths, University of London and a BA in Liberal Arts and Film Studies from King's College London. His criticism on visual art, performance and cinema has appeared in *Wales Arts Review*, *O'r Pedwar Gwynt* and *Barn*.

Ruqaya Izzidien is an Iraqi-Welsh writer and graduate of Durham University. As a journalist, her work has appeared in the *New York Times*, *Al Jazeera*, the *New Statesman*, *The New Arab*, *The National*, and the BBC. Her debut novel, *The Watermelon Boys*, set in WW1 Baghdad, was published by Hoopoe Fiction in 2018 and received a Betty Trask Award for first-time novelists under 35.

Bethan Jones-Arthur is a bisexual, bilingual Valleys native with a penchant for whisky, chicken wings, and French and Saunders. A journalism graduate, she works in communications and writes plays, stories and essays on the side. She now lives in Cardiff with her partner and a cat called Mistar Augustus. If she's not at home in her jamas, you can find Bethan at a comedy gig or street food festival. This is Bethan's first 'proper' published work, though she did win a competition in *Cip* magazine once.

Derwen Morfayel is a fiction writer. Born in Spain and bred in Wales, she tends to write in English but would enjoy exploring her Spanish creativity in future. She has a degree in Creative Writing and an M.Phil. for which she completed her first novel. Her work has been published in literary magazines and journals including stories in *The Lonely Crowd, Silvae, Halo*, the webzine *Ink, Sweat & Tears* and more. Recent work includes a stream-of-consciousness piece as part of USW's 'Interior Monologues' exhibition and zine featuring collaborations between artists and writers. Currently she is working on short stories.

Grug Muse is a PhD student at the Welsh department in Swansea University. She won the chair at the 2013 Urdd eisteddfod and her work has appeared in publications such as *O'r Pedwar Gwynt, Poetry Wales* and *Wales Arts Review*. She is co-founder and co-editor of *Y Stamp*, a Welsh language Arts magazine; and in 2017 published her first volume of poetry, *Ar Ddisberod* with *Cyhoeddiadau Barddas*.

Dafydd C Reeves was born and bred in Brecon, Powys. He has a keen interest in the fantastic; from comics, videogames and fantasy novels to Welsh mythology and local folklore. He also reads non-fiction and watches documentaries about history, religion and philosophy. He is a bilingual singer-songwriter and Instapoet in English and in Welsh. Following a generous critique of his entry to a Welsh fantasy short story competition for the National Eisteddfod 2019 he has redoubled his efforts and is working on writing stories set in his fantasy world.

Ranjit Saimbi is a writer, highly commended in the 2018 Bridport Prize for his other works include 'The Cornershop Kid' and 'My Guy Jay'. His family are of the Ugandan Asian diaspora, expelled from Uganda in the 1970s, and now firmly settled in the UK. He was born in Cardiff where he spent his formative years, winning a scholarship to Eton College and graduating from Durham University with a first-class honours degree in English Literature. He previously practiced as a lawyer at an international law firm, specialising in corporate law. He currently lives in London and works in the tech industry.

Nasia Sarwar-Skuse is a solicitor and writer. As a bilingual Urdu and English speaker, working with words has been integral to the articulation and creation of her work. Nasia has recently completed an MA in Creative Writing at Cardiff University. She is interested in the presence of authenticity in literature by ethnic voices and its intersections with diaspora, gender and memory. In 2017, Nasia was shortlisted by Penguin Random house for the WriteNow programme. Nasia is a recipient of Literature Wales Bursary for emerging writers and is working on her first novel.

Ricky Stevenson is a writer from Swansea, and since achieving an MA in Creative Writing from Swansea University a selection of his comedy plays have been performed by the Fluellen Theatre Company, including 'Are we there, Yeti?' and 'Jackpot!' Ricky lives with cerebral palsy, and is a transitional boccia player in Team GB. He has been part of the team for over a year now, and it's been a huge learning experience, full of drama, doubt and confusion – the perfect recipe for comedy!

Kandace Siobhan Walker is a writer and filmmaker. She has collaborated on film projects with IdeasTap, DAZED and the Institute of Contemporary Arts. Her work has appeared in *The Guardian*, *Protoype* and *The Good Journal*. Her short story 'Deep Heart' won the 2019 Guardian 4th Estate BAME Short Story Prize. She lives in Powys.

Josh Weeks is a writer from Caldicot, south Wales, who is currently studying for a PhD in Latin American literature at the University of Amsterdam. His previous work has been longlisted for the Bath Flash Fiction Award, included in the *Cheval Anthology* of young Welsh writers, and published by *Ellipsis Zine* and *Five 2 One* magazine. He has a chapbook forthcoming with Amsterdam-based indie publisher, Otherwhere.

Sarah Younan is Lebanese-German. She was born in Germany, raised in Kenya and has been living in Wales for 10 years now. As a mixed-race woman who grew up in Kenya, she draws on her experiences and writes to challenge how non-Western experiences are still romanticised and reduced to easily graspable stereotypes and to question tropes in writing about the 'other'. A formerly starving artist, she has a PhD in ceramics, and does film programming and production with Watch Africa Cymru. She is an Arts Council Trustee and holding down a day job at Amgueddfa Cymru-National Museum Wales.

Acknowledgements

All reasonable efforts have been made to trace the authors of the quotes used within *Just So You Know*.

Thanks are given to the following:

Copyright © 2017 by the Board of Regents of the University of Nebraska. Reproduced from *The January Children* by Safia Elhillo by kind permission of the University of Nebraska Press.

Copyright © 1991 by Stad Gerallt Lloyd Owen from *Cilmeri a cherddi eraill*. Reprinted by kind permission of Mirain Llwyd.

Copyright © by Ijeoma Umebinyuo from *Questions for Ada*. Reprinted by kind permission of the author.

PARTHIAN Fiction

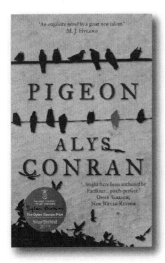

Pigeon

Alys Conran
ISBN 978-1-910901-23-6
£8.99 • Paperback

Winner of Wales Book of the Year
Winner of The Rhys Davies Award

'An exquisite novel by a great new talent.' – M.J. Hyland

Ironopolis

Glen James Brown
ISBN 978-1-912681-09-9
£9.99 • Paperback

Shortlisted for the Orwell Prize for Political Fiction

'A triumph' – *The Guardian*

'The most accomplished working-class novel of the last few years.' – *Morning Star*

PARTHIAN   Fiction

The Levels

Helen Pendry
ISBN 978-1-912109-40-1
£8.99 • Paperback

'...an important new literary voice.'
– Wales Arts Review

Shattercone

Tristan Hughes
ISBN 978-1-912681-47-1
£8.99 • Paperback

On *Hummingbird*:
'Superbly accomplished... Hughes prose is
startling and luminous' – *Financial Times*

Hello Friend
We Missed You

Richard Owain Roberts
ISBN 978-1-912681-49-5
£9.99 • Paperback

'The Welsh David Foster Wallace'
– Srdjan Srdic

The Blue Tent

Richard Gwyn
ISBN 978-1-912681-28-0
£10 • Paperback

'One of the most satisfying, engrossing and
perfectly realised novels of the year.'
– *The Western Mail*

PARTHIAN

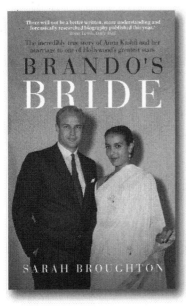

Brando's Bride
SARAH BROUGHTON

The incredibly true story of Anna Kashfi and her marriage to one of Hollywood's greatest stars

ISBN 978-1-912681-27-3 • £10

"There will not be a better written, more understanding and forensically researched biography published this year."
– Roger Lewis, *The Daily Mail*

I, Eric Ngalle
ERIC NGALLE

One Man's Journey Crossing Continents from Africa to Europe

ISBN 978-1-912109-10-4 • £9.99

"Powerful and challenging..."
– Ifor Ap Glyn

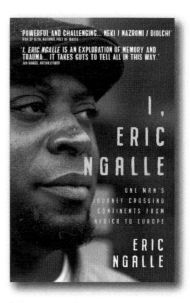